Horses

[1001]
[photos]

[1O01] photos

Horses

© 2006 Éditions Solar, an imprint of Place des Éditeurs
© 2007 Rebo International, b.v., Lisse, The Netherlands

This edition printed in 2009.

Text: Corinne Francois Huart and Ségolene Roy
Photography: Yves Lanceau and furrytails.nl
Coordination: Isabelle Raimond
Graphic design: Gwénaël Le Cossec
Translation: First Edition Translations Ltd, Cambridge, UK
Typesetting: A.R. Garamond, Prague, Czech Republic

ISBN: 978 90 366 2251 6

Horses
[1001]
[photos

REBO
PUBLISHERS

Contents

Wild horses

Social horses

Racing horses

Dressage horses

Jumping horses

Recreational horses

Game horses

Exhibition horses

Work horses

Horse careers

Horses in the wild

Wild horses

The Camargue horse,
known to the Phoenicians,
is one of the oldest breeds
in the world.

The Camargue is one of the oldest breeds in the world. Some experts suggest it is of Asian origin; others think that the Solutré horses are its predecessors as fossils were discovered in the archaeological excavation area of the same name in the Saône-et-Loire region. The only sure thing is that the Camargue have lived in isolation in the delta of the Rhôna River for several thousand years.

You will not see it elsewhere; its breeding area has never crossed the triangular area comprised of the vertexes of Montpellier, Tarascon and Fos. The horse inherited its ampleness from its birthplace of marshes and sparse vegetation. The horse has strong pace, an indubitable instinct and has excellently adapted to its environment. They are the essential helpers of famous Camargue guardians who bred them in herds called manadas in order to collect and guard livestock. Provence, which is very proud of its small white horses, invites them to all of its traditional feast days – you can see them every year in the parades which take place at the festivals in Nîmes and Arles and at the gypsy fair in Saintes-Maries-de-la-Mer. They are valued for their mild and serene disposition and are also used for tourist riding. Due to their small stature, they elicit confidence in beginners.

From the body constitution point of view, a Camargue horse is somewhat thickset with muscular and strong legs. They have deep chests and short loins. Their head is wide with lively eyes and the distinct small ears are very nimble. The foals are dark and at six to seven years of age they begin

The beautiful white Camargue

to change to a grey color. It is rare to see a chestnut colored Camargue horse. The guardians, in order to improve the breed, used to castrate the less appealing stallions during the annual gathering.

In the fifties, the breed almost disappeared. The breeding was successfully revived thanks to the riding tourism and the registering the Camargue horse in the stud book in 1968.

[1] The territory of the Camargue horses is the marshy areas close to the salty lakes.
[2] One of the characteristic features of the Camargue horses is their white mane.
[3] The Camargue horse is usually considered to be a pony.

[1] The Camargue horse is small; its height does not exceed 145 cm (5 feet).
[2] The coat of the Camargue horse is white, grey or dappled.
[3] The Camargue horse is frequently accompanied by birds such as herons and egrets.

[4] The Camargue horse is a rustic horse. It is one of a few breeds able to graze in water.
[5] The Camargue horses are free-bred.

13

[1-2] The Camargue horse can withstand long fasting, resist unfavorable weather conditions and travel long distances.

[3] The Guardians ride on the Camargue horses to gather the herds of bulls.

[4] In summer, the Camargue horses are neither afraid of hot days, horseflies or mosquitoes. [5] The Camargue horses still run freely outdoors, they do not know what stables are.

15

[1] The tourist economy of the Saintes-Maries-de-la-mer area is based on the riding of the Camargue horses.
[2] The Camargue horse must be in permanent motion because there are few substantial pastures in its area.
[3] The stallions of the Camargue horse are also known as "grignoun."

[4-5] The Camargue horses are usually born without human assistance; they are captured and branded when they are about one year old.
[6] The Camargue foals remain in the company of a single stallion all year long.

[1-2 and right page]
The Camargue horse was the riding horse of the Camisards of the Cevennes region. Later on, Napoleon used the horses for his army and around 1865, the horse proved to be a useful carrier during the construction of the Suez Canal.

[1] The owners of the flocks are very fond of their horses: when the best ones die, they are buried standing with their saddle on.
[2] A tamed Camargue horse is a mild mannered horse, well inured to the saddle.

[3] Saddling of a still wild Camargue horse is an opportunity for celebrations commemorating the rodeos of the Wild West.

[4] A monada consists of at least four free-bred breeding mares.
[5] A young Camargue foal usually has a very dark coat which turns light at around four to five years old.

The Tarpan is of Eastern European origin and the Przewalski horse comes from the Mongolian steppes on the border with the Gobi desert. These two wild horses, often wanted for their meat and hunted by breeders envying their pastures or as a work force, can only thank some recent protective measures for their survival.

Despite this, the animals have not returned to the wild. The Przewalski horses first survived only in zoos. The program for the re-implantation of the breed that was launched in 1992 has allowed them to successively gain their freedom again. The extinction of the wild Tarpan was averted by re-breeding in Poland. Over the years, both breeds have retained the features of their predecessors. They are robust, with heavy heads and strong legs. The Przewalski horse, with a height of about 120 – 140 cm (4–5 feet), has a slender back, short shin bones and an upright mane similar to zebras. The Tarpan horse is slimmer but smaller and its predominant features are the back strip similar to a mule and the zebra like stripes on the legs.

The Mustang is the offspring of domesticated horses brought by Spanish conquistadores in the 16th century. It seems some animals escaped their captivity and multiplied at liberty. Red Indian tribes and cowboys managed to get them successfully under control but a small number still remained wild. Today, they are protected. Their height does not exceed 150 cm, they have strong legs with a hollow back. They are frugal and durable with strong pace. Contrary to the Tarpan, which is timid, and can be uncompromising, the Mustang is obedient after taming and makes a good saddle horse.

Tarpan, Przewalski and Mustang

[Left page and the photo down] The Przewalski horse, formerly known as the Tarpan, ran freely across large areas of Central Asia and Western Europe. The cave paintings in Lascaux in France and Altamira in Spain provide evidence of this. The horse has not changed much since the Stone Age. The hostile environment and its animosity towards different breeds have protected it against crossbreeding.

[1-2] The Tarpan which became a hunting animal, no longer exists in the wild: the last one was probably seen in 1966. Today, Tarpans live dispersed over 120 zoological gardens or private paddocks across four continents.

[3-4] The Tarpan breeds well in captivity and there are more than one thousand horses of that breed in the world today.

27

[1-2] Mustangs are the offspring of horses brought by the Spanish conquistadores in the 16th century and who then escaped back to the wild. Originally, they were the cross-breed of the Andalusian and Barb horses.
[3] Carefully approaching a Mustang stallion.

[4] An Andalusian Mustang foal
[5] Sale of Mustangs in Montana.
[6] The sale of Mustangs dates back to the times before the arrival of settlers to the US. Today, as in the past, they are auctioned.

[1] The name "mustang" comes from the Spanish *mesteño* and Mexican *monstenco*; they mean "wild" or "roaming."
[2] A Mustang bearing a coat called the "blue roan."

[3] In 1900, there were over a million mustangs; today, hardly 100,000 have survived.

[4-5-6] Some American Indian tribes succeeded in taming the Mustangs in order to break them in and to ride them. However in most cases, they bought or stole already tamed horses from other tribes, settlers or the cavalry.

Social horses

The sturdy and strong Norwegian Fjord was a traditional Viking horse which was used as an agricultural helper for wood towing and ploughing, as a means of transport and as a war horse. The Vikings also organized gambling based mortal combat of the Fjords.

The Fjord is a charming pony of calm, lively and brave disposition which is now bred in Northern Europe, France, Great Britain and in the USA. The horse has adapted to hard living conditions, can instinctively walk well on slippery and steep paths and therefore, is an ideal horse for tourist riding. Its amiable nature makes it a very popular social horse. It has a dun or mousy grey color and can grow up to 145 cm (5 feet) tall.

The Shetland comes from the islands of the same name but today is bred worldwide. Traditionally, it has been used as a work horse on fields or in coal mines. It is strong and small and therefore an excellent riding horse for children. Its color ranges from black to chestnut, bay, brown and pinto. As far as its temperament is concerned, it seems stubborn and quick tempered although very amiable. Despite not having the fame of being suitable for cross-breeding, it is one of the predecessors of the American Shetland, an excellent fine and elegant pony for teaming and also of the Argentinean falabella, a miniature pony whose height does not exceed 80 cm.

As the food resources on the Shetland Islands are poor, the pony height evolved by oscillating from 95 to 105 cm. Due to the hard environment, the Shetland gained its legendary sturdiness and resilience. It has a compact, massive and symmetrical

Norwegian Fjord and Shetland

body. The limbs and joints are strong and it has a thick and dense tail with a mane which protects against cold in the winter.

[1] The Vikings used the Fjord horses for ploughing and wood towing.
[2] A foal of the Fjord horse stands up and drinks from its mother 30 minutes after birth.

[3] The mares of the Fjord horses foal after an 11 month gestation period. Despite this they are sexually mature between 12 and 18 months although they do not reproduce earlier than after three years of breeding.

[1-2] The Shetland is one of the smallest ponies: it grows 90 – 105 cm (the smallest is only 65 cm). As far as weight is concerned, they can weigh between 150 – 180 kg (330–400 ponds).

[3] Foaling usually occurs in the pastures between April and June.
[4] Despite their obedient nature, the Shetland stallions are not suitable for riding.

39

[1] The coat of the Shetland ponies is bicolor in many cases.
[2] The Shetland ponies, mainly the stallions, have a mane covering their eyes.

[3] The Shetland mares have very strong maternal feelings.

[4 - 7] Very small Shetland ponies were successively bred and are now called Mini-Shetlands. They are social horses or riding horses for children.

41

The Appaloosa breed was bred
by the American Indians from
the Nez-Percé tribe.

There are about twenty main pony breeds, many of which come from Anglo-Saxon countries. The English Exmoor is characterized by gibbous eyes, spotted nostrils, a wide forehead and its large size, which enables riding both for children and adults. The New Forest Pony which comes from the south of England is characterized by its height, fast pace and its mild and amiable nature.

The Scottish Highland Pony, which is a very old breed, has experienced much cross-breeding over the years. Cross-breeding with thoroughbreds results in excellent horses for long rides and racing horses. The Welsh Mountain is one of the most attractive ponies as it is strong, elegant, and clever (which is unusual) and therefore, makes a good racing and team horse. It paved the way for Welsh breeds such as the Welsh Pony Section B and the Welsh Cob, which is both an excellent companion and a good riding horse; however the best results are achieved in hurdle running. The Icelandic, a close relative of the Norwegian Fjord, boasts a pleasant pace called "tilt" while being stupendously comfortable for saddle seating. Argentina is the home country to two especially playful and lovely ponies: the Criollo with a compact and firm silhouette and the Falabella, a pygmoid horse with a height not exceeding 60 cm. Although the pony cannot be saddled, it can tow light carriages. As far as France is represented, there is the Landes pony, a rustic but elegant pony. Its finesse and firmness make it

Other pony breeds

good for teaming. The French Saddle Pony is the result of much cross-breeding which has not given any special feature to the horse unless the predilection for the saddle is considered. You can see it in the racing, riding and dressage competitions.

42

[1] The settlers named these horses after the Palouse brook close to where the Nez-Percés tribe resided.

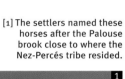

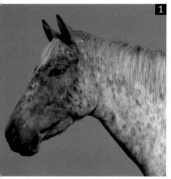

[2-3] The "Appaloosa" word is both the name of the horse breed and the spotted coat color.

[4] Wild pony of the Dulmen breed.
[5-6] The Icelandic arrived in Iceland with the Vikings more than 1,000 years ago and never cross-bred with any other breed. Its speciality is the five natural paces: walk, trot, canter, tilt and amble.

45

[1-2] The food for the Icelandic is modest. Keeping this horse is easy; it can carry heavy loads and calmly cooperates with the rider.

[3] For over a thousand years, the Icelandic breed has been a pedigree because in 930, the Iceland borders closed to all horse imports. From that moment on, the blood of these horses has never mixed with any outsider and therefore, it has retained the features of its predecessors. On this tough island located in the polar area, the horse has had to harden and adapt to the environment.

[1] For centuries, the Icelandic was imported into Britain to work in mines where its bravery, resilience and obedience were appreciated. [2] The Siciliano horse is a local Sicilian breed.

[3] The Falabella breed was bred by the Falabella family at the end of the 19th century in Reero de Roca hacienda close to Buenos Aires, Argentina. It was bred by cross-breeding small thoroughbreds with small Shetland ponies. [Right page] Approximately 75,000 horses live in Iceland, and are mainly used for breeding or riding.

[1-2] The Falabella is often considered a social animal; however its power and physical features require at least the minimum riding knowledge.

[3] The New Forest was named after the forest in the county of Hampshire in Southern England where it lives in the wild.

[4] The resilient and undemanding New Forest pony can adapt to any breeding areas. When imported to France, it was bred mainly in Normandy and in the Berry area. Roughly 40 percent of the stud farms are situated in Normandy; the others operate deep in the Loira Valley and in the southeast of the country.

[Left page 1 – 4]
The birthplace of the New Forest Pony is the southern part of Great Britain after which it is named. It lives here in the wild in moorland, thickets and marshes.

53

[1-2] The New Forest Pony first came to France in the sixties and immediately fascinated the breeders with its peaceful nature, coolness, resilience and obedience.

[3-4] In 1874, a foal was born, the offspring of Arabian horse and a local mare, in the village of Hafling near Merano in the Northern Italy. The foal was named Folie and he became the very first stallion of the Haflinger breed.

54

[5] The breeding New Forest ponies are called "studs" instead of "forests" when living in the wild.

[1-2] In Italy, the Haflings are called Avelignese.

[3] The Haflings can adapt to any climatic conditions and can be bred both in stables and outdoors. They are extraordinarily fertile thanks to very easy foaling. The easy breeding and riding is considerably helped by their nature and temperament.

[Left page] The Haflinger breed is suitable both for saddling and teaming.
[1] The Flabella pony buckskin, i.e. with the deerskin color coat.
[2] The Norwegian Fjord is a small, brave, modest and resilient horse originating from Norway. The figure shows a stallion.

To have a privileged companion, to devote everyday care, to groom, feed and to go for rides – all these romantic images can be visualized by any rider or a child wanting to own a horse. In truth, it is much more frustrating to visit your animal weekly for just a couple of hours in a strange stable rather than to have it with you at home.

However, don't forget that a horse at home requires material resources and requires a lot of your available time. A horse has a stable nature and high spatial needs. It should have a suitable environment available so as not to be bored. A box that is too narrow must be avoided as should insufficient rides and loneliness. The first necessity is a companion. Not a sheep or goat as can frequently be seen but a horse or a pony as both the equidaes understand each other well. If no meadow is available to have a good frolic, the box must be big enough for the horse to turn, stretch or lay down. It is a good idea to keep the upper part of the box door still open (except in bad weather conditions) in order to allow the horse to watch its masters doing their work in the yard. After all these conditions are met, the box must be prepared for the horse: bring the manure, check that no water or fodder is missing in the stable. The horse's health should be taken care of as well: it must be regularly vaccinated and have its teeth checked; administer anthelmintics twice a year so as to avoid parasites. As horses are sensitive to the cold, they must be kept indoors and covered in winter. The work is very demanding but rewarding. The more care and attention the horse gets, the more the horse sticks to its masters.

Domestic horses

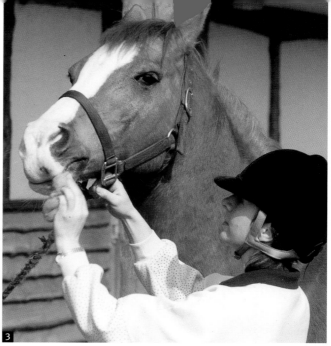

[1] Harnesses should be
well maintained.
[2] Clean the hooves
before going for any rides.
[3] Clean the bit-stressed
muzzle thoroughly.
[4] Learning to care for
a horse is as equally
important as learning
to ride a horse.

[5] Horses quickly learn to recognize their carer. They share affection.
[6] Regular mane and tail combing avoids tangling.
[7] The horse should be groomed daily.

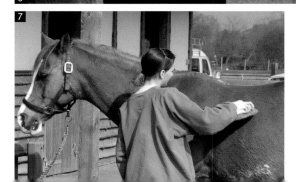

[Page left and down] Very young riders can attend the races. Suitable equipment is essential, such as the correct riding hat, saddle and stirrups adapted to the height of the rider. Everything needs to be checked and correctly set up before saddling.

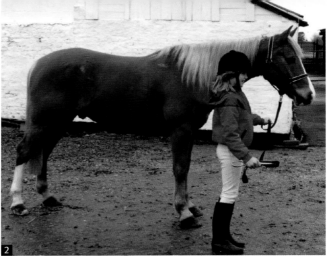

[1] There are as many saddle types as there are riding styles.
[2] A horse being held while leaving its box.
[3] Regular replacement of bedding protects the animal against parasites and diseases.

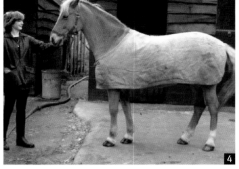

[4] In winter or after intensive riding, the horse is usually covered up.
[5] The final grooming before saddling.
[6] The horse is ready.

[1] The horses love the company of children.
[2] The foals need a lot of stroking.

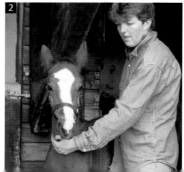

Social horses

[3] The saddles are heavy and
transported in large baskets.
[4] Children waiting for their
riding lesson.

69

The Arabian horse is one of the oldest breeds in the world.

T his horse is extraordinarily capable, brave, fast, the star of the equidae and one of the most sought after and admired horses. Some races are reserved only for them. The origin of the horse is mysterious but we know that its resilience and power resulted from its hard life with the Bedouins in the scorched areas of the Middle East stretching from the Tigris River to Yemen.

The breeders were warriors and methodically bred the horses to produce a fast and determined horse capable of carrying the rider for long periods of time – it was a real war horse. The horse breed was used in the Muslim invasion, which resulted in its presence in the Iberian Peninsula and throughout the rest of Europe. Westerners used them for founding "pure" tribes and for improving the other breeds. This was mainly used for the breeding of English and English-Arab thoroughbreds. The breed influenced others as well where it improved their nerve impulse and resistance.

The horse is of small stature and has extraordinary aesthetic features. The horse is very fine, with an exquisite head and small agile ears giving it a clever appearance; moreover, it has a body that especially shows the reason for its highly carried tail: it has 17 vertebras, 5 lumbar vertebras and 16 tail vertebras instead of the usual 16, 6 and 18. It is a pleasant social horse which achieves excellent results in horse racing, horse teams and in tourism riding. It has a reddish, brown or grey colour and a beautiful, long and fluttering mane. The Arabian horse has an excellent temperament which results in it being a very good social breed. It is a well looked after breed for recreation and

Arabian thoroughbred horses

tourism riding and can also pull light loads. The breed still plays an important role in improving further horse breeds.

[1-2-3] An Egyptian thoroughbred was the predecessor of the horse used by the Bedouins on the Arabian Peninsula during raids into the camps of the surrounding tribes. These raids often included the stealing of horses. It was necessary to get out quickly and shake off the pursuers after the raids so a fast horse was necessary.

[4-5-6] In most cases, only mares were used for the raids because of their quietness and ability to approach silently without neighing. Therefore, their owners valued them highly and formed close relations with them and sometimes, the mares were even allowed to hide in their tents.

73

[1-2-3] The Arabian thorough-breds existed 2000 years B.C. in Egypt. Some of the frescos attest to this by showing an Arabian horse teamed with a carriage.

[4 and 7] The Arabian thoroughbred is a small horse 144 – 155 cm high. Most frequently, the coat is grey, chestnut and dark brown and sometimes black as well.

[1-2-3] The Arabian horse is valued for its very dispassionate nature remains an ideal companion for leisure time and riding.

[4] The Ahagya is a Hungarian version of the Arabian thoroughbred.
[5-6] Today, the Arabian horses are bred rather for their breed and beauty. In other words, the Arabian thoroughbred is considered to be a breed improver.

[3] The Shagya Arabian was a war horse of the Austrian-Hungarian armed forces and then as a ceremonial horse at the Viennese imperial court.

[1-2-4-5-6-7] Like all horses, an Arabian mare has one foal after 11 months of gravidity.

[1-2-3 and right page]
The thoroughbred Arabian
horses have special physical
characteristics. They have
17 back and 5 lumbar vertebras
instead of usual respective
18 and 6.

Racing horses

In the past, the English Parliament did not sit in session on the day of the very popular Grand National race.

The obstacle races include three disciplines: cross country racing, hurdling and steeplechasing, which is the royal and by far the most effective discipline. It originated in 1752 in Ireland as the result of a bet between two chase lovers. Two riders decided to race the seven kilometer length between the steeples of Buttevant and Saint-Léger.

And that is how the name steeplechase, the name of the race, originated. Shortly thereafter, similar races took place across Great Britain. In France, the "steeple chases" were introduced in 1830 and from the 1870s, they took place at the hippodrome in Auteuil. The most famous country chase, the "Grand Steeple-Chase de Paris" still takes place there today. Today, the steeplechase length is 3,000 – 7,000 meters and requires not only speed but also endurance because of several imposing hurdles (at least eight). In most cases, this includes streams, 115 cm high bar hurdles surrounded by barriers to achieve an overall width of 170 cm, full ditches, bordered soil hills with hurdles, oxer jumps, ditches bordered

by hurdles at least three meters wide and open ditches (ditches followed by a hurdle). Some hurdles, dreaded more than others, are world famous today, such as Beecher's Brook at the Grand National in Liverpool, which is at first a 60 cm high hill upwards and then 160 cm downwards so the horses need to make a great jump. The river in

The steeplechase

Auteuil is also famous for its width of 440 cm with a barrier in front of it so the horses must make a six meter plus long jump. The fabulous racecourse of the Grand National is known as the most difficult in the whole world – it is over 7,200 meters and has a minimum of 30 hurdles.

[1-2] Getting across the river is a very sensitive moment both for the horse and rider.

1

2

3 [3] During steeplechases, the horses must jump hurdles more than 100 cm high.

[4-5-6] The Grand National in Liverpool is known by its difficulty; there are many falls which are protested against by the animal protection leagues.

1 [1-2] *The Chair* is the largest and most difficult hurdle at the Grand National in Liverpool.

[3-4] *The Chair* located in the end of the racecourse usually results in many dangerous falls.

[1] Previously, a taut rope across the track was used to start the horse race. Today, each horse is in a starting stall.
[2] The drawings on the riding caps and the tunics of the riders determine their owner.

[3] As soon as the door opens, the horses dart forward.
[4-5] Hurdle racing is highly spectacular, especially when all the riders jump the hurdles at the same time.

[1-2] Steeplechase races are organized in many countries and on the snow as well, such as in St. Moritz in Switzerland.

[3] The steeplechase in Whaddon Chase is famous.

[4] The starting stalls allow all the horses to dart forward at the same time and avoid jostling or impeding other racers.

A racing horse undergoes intensive training from its early youth. At approximately 18 months old, the horse leaves its native stud farm and goes into the hands of a trainer, who with the help of a stable-boy, takes care of its training, education and the learning of all three paces. Firstly, long rides at a trot or a walk are made to make the horse stronger.

Then the speed, breath and endurance training starts with morning canters and running the yearling over short distances at a moderate pace. Successively, the track becomes longer and the speed increases. This trains the horse for sprinting – the horse must run at full speed over a short distance. The best care is given to the horse in the stable where special attention is paid to its feed as it must help this athlete get fit. The horses can start racing at two years of age. The races for this age category take place on a racecourse with a maximum distance of 1,600 meters. At three years, the distance may be as much as 3,100 meters. Depending on their abilities, the horses are trained for local races or the Grand National chases. If they lack speed but have a great jumping talent, they are prepared for the hurdle races and then for the steeplechase; in the latter, horses younger than five years can rarely be seen.

Although the thoroughbreds are bred worldwide, the qualities expected from them differ in individual countries.

The laws of discipline

For example in the USA, races can be shorter than 1,500 meters and hence, good sprinters are preferred. On the contrary in Europe, they race at between 2,000 – 4,000 meters and therefore, better endurance is required. Hence, the training of the thoroughbreds requires slightly different methods on both sides of the Atlantic.

[1-2] The Derby attracts many spectators who most often gather at the point where the course curves and the view is the most exciting.

[3] Many races take place at Sandown.
[4] Opposite the terraces, the final sprint of Royal Ascot is under way.

1

2 [1-2 and left page] At the famous ski resort of St. Moritz (Switzerland) there are many horse related events in winter: flat or harness trotting races as well as polo matches.

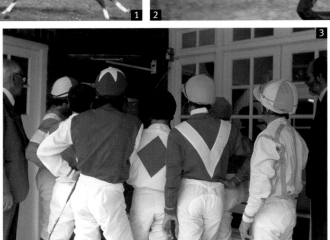

[1-2] Warming up is very important for a racing horse; this is done in the very early morning.
[3] Jockeys are great athletes who must be on a strict diet.

[4] During the steeplechase, the jockeys wear goggles for protection against branches, soil and mud from competitor's horses.

[1] The large breeders have stables where all boxes lead to a central inner court used for guiding the horses.

[2 and 5] The stable-boys set out with the horses early in the morning for a foggy ride and then quickly gallop back to the stables.

[1] During the ride, the stable boys let the horses nibble fresh grass.
[2] On nice days, the mares and foals are taken out to a meadow.
[Right page] The box doors are open in order to let air flow in and to allow the horses to poke their heads out.

The English thoroughbred horse, the result of cross-breeding of British mares and Arabian stallions, is the success of the selective breeding field. They have strong hind-quarters allowing flexible and penetrative movement, long and resilient legs, a small head and a narrow but firm neck; the body in general is elegant while also athletic and built for speed.

The breed is relatively new, it originated between the 17th and 18th century. At the beginning of the three contemporary family lines of Matchem, Herod and Eclipse, there were three Arabian stallions imported between 1690 and 1729 to England: Byerley Turk, Darley Arabian and Godolphin Arabian. Eclipse was a legendary horse who won twenty six times in twenty six starts. In the 17th century, the racing world began to structure and codify. The pioneer of this was England where King Charles the Second was a passionate rider. During the meetings, the horses started to be sorted according to their sex and age; at the beginning of the next century, the first hippodromes deserving of their names emerged; the first one was opened in Newmarket in the territory of the royal hunting ground; the still existing Jockey Club was founded here to oversee riding activities. Later, great races such as The Derby in Epson, The Saint-Léger and The Oaks were organized. England was the trendsetter and offered a model of infrastructure which inspired many other countries. In the 19th century, the English inspired French Jockey Club was established and

Saga of the thoroughbreds

famous hippodromes were built there and used for famous races such as the Prix de Diane, Poule d'essai and the Grand Prix de Paris. Flat racing, hurdle racing and trotting racing are all distinguished between. The trotting races use those horses cross-bred with the thoroughbreds. The best is the French Trotter, the offspring of English stallions and Normandy mares.

3 [1-2-3] One of the key moments of the Grand National in Liverpool is the river jumping.

[4-5-6] The racing horses for steeplechasing must be fast, agile and must not be afraid of jumping the hurdles.

1 **2**

3 [1-2] Usually, the race horses are so close together that a head decides the race winner. [3] In England, horse racing is very popular; people bet a lot of money on their favorites.

[4] The starting stalls are wheeled and transported by tractors depending on the race length.
[5] At the finish, the jockey slowly loosens the reins so as to calmly stop the horse.
[6] The final spurt.

3 [1-2-3] The Grand National attracts many riders and spectators as the hurdles are very spectacular here.

112

[4-5] Before the start, the horses and the riders walk in front of the terraces. They are guided by helpers so as not to stray.

113

[1-2] The jockeys want the most power from the horses in the final straight.

114

[3] The flat race at Ascot is famous throughout England and the best gallopers race there. The racecourse is located in a huge park with century old trees.

[1-2-3] After the race, the winners meet their owners. The men wear top hats and the women wear extravagant hats.

[4-5] The jockeys lie on the horses and horsewhip them in order to cross the finish line first.

117

118

[1-2-3] The Ascot terrace was built 150 years ago. It is situated opposite the home stretch and has been reconstructed many times. In the highest part are private VIP cabins, especially reserved for members of the royal family.

Dressage
horses

The favorite horses of the
big riding schools are the
white-coated Lipizzans.

The very first treatise on the riding art was compiled by Xenophon, the Greek general, philosopher and historian (4th century B.C.). The treatise was an undisputed source of inspiration for the great Italian Renaissance masters who established the tradition of academic riding in Europe.

Truly, their attempts were motivated by the military requirements of the continuously improving cavalry and the excellent controlling of the war horses but at the same time, a sophisticated art, of which the basic principle was to return to the horse the qualities it had in the wild, was developed. The schools jumps, which are the curvet, the croupade and the capriole conform to natural horse jumps known as the rearing, the buck and the jump.

In the academy of art and elegance

France had dominated this discipline for many years. François Robichon de la Guérinière (1687-1751), who was the director of the riding school of Tuileries for over thirty years, founded the "French style," the fine, easy and natural guiding of a horse and came up with the practices still used today such as "travers" and "renvers," tail to the wall and hand to the wall, "shoulder-in," and stretching exercises.

Today, two institutions rule the world of the academic dressage. The Spanish Riding School of Vienna retained the classic riding art of Renaissance without any changes. The horse of court is the white Lipizzan, a sturdy while elegant horse resulting from the cross-breeding of Andalusian stallions and local mares. The only competitor to the Vienna school is the Cadre noir de Saumur established in 1764. The teachings of Earl Aure of Baucher and L'Hotte, who managed the school in the 19th century are still maintained there.

[1] The biggest studs of the Lipizzans are in Austria, Slovenia, Croatia and Hungary.

[2] The Andalusian embodies nobility, grace and beauty, allied to power.
[3] The Lipizzan mares go with their foals to the paddock.

[4] The pure white coat is a feature of the breed.
[5] The breeding of the Lipizzans is most intensive in the Oak Mountains in the north of Hungary.

[1-2-3] The Spanish Riding School of Vienna is the only institution in the world which today still retains and cultivates the classic riding high art of the Renaissance times without changing it.

[4-5-6] After years of training, the horse and rider are so close together that they form a unit. The movements of the Lipizzans are in great accord with the music and the audience has an unforgettable experience.

127

[1-2-3] The gala performances take place in the great environment of the Vienna Imperial Palace designed by the baroque architect, Joseph Emmanuel Fischer von Erlach. At that time, young aristocrats would learn their horse riding there.

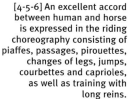

[4-5-6] An excellent accord between human and horse is expressed in the riding choreography consisting of piaffes, passages, pirouettes, changes of legs, jumps, courbettes and caprioles, as well as training with long reins.

129

[1] In Hungary, the Lipizzans are bred in the wild.
[2] A foal of the Andalusian horse has a coat that becomes darker later.

[3] The foals of the Lipizzans are born with a black mane that later turns grey and then white at adult age.
[4] The coat of some Andalusian horses is very light but the most sought after are the black and dark brown Andalusians.

T he goal of dressage is make the horse "quiet, acquiescent, nimble and flexible" as well as "confident, attentive and sharp," states the guide book of the International Riding Federation. Each and every rider, regardless of whether they like to race or jump, should familiarize themselves with the basics of this discipline so as to understand their horse much better.

The dressage competitions, that appeared early in the 20th century, take place on a 60 x 20 m track based on music either as a free or dressage test. The jury classifies the figures, the stopping and changing of pace; they also judge the rider, the horse and how they develop as a pair. The low level dressage tests contain easy practices such as stopping, reversing and changing direction in three paces; the horse must express its frankness and impetus and the rider must especially have good saddle seating as well as the correct leg position. The Olympic competition is for the top level riders. They have to show grace above the ground, not jumps, reserved for the riders from Saumuru and Vienna and a complete practice requiring years of training such as the piaffe, a very collected, cadenced, high stepping diagonal movement evoking the impression of on the spot trotting, the passage, slow high trotting or a change of leg in the air. The horse

Required dressage figures

must be in a straight position and on the bit, i.e. no resistance to the rider is allowed. The correct dressage horses are elegant, loose, amenable and alert. The best horses are the studs from Germany, Holland and Russia.

[1-2-3] Dressage allows the achievement of purity and the excellence of the pace. When the competition horses know how to rot, they are then trained in more complex paces such as the piaffé or the passage.

[4-5-6] The rider's body bearing is equally important to the pace of the horse. The trunk must be kept straight.

[1-2-3-4] The racecourse in Goodwood (southern England) hosts many riding competitions as well as automobile events.

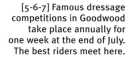

[5-6-7] Famous dressage competitions in Goodwood take place annually for one week at the end of July. The best riders meet here.

[1-2-3 and right side]
The most visited rides are the competitions in Badminton, England. The riders wear a special riding hat in the form of the bowler.

[1-2] A reward for the riders is the participation in the dressage competition in Badminton.
[3] Annually, Goodwood attracts thousands of visitors.

[4-5-6-7] The appearance of the horse and rider is almost equally important for the victory as the sports performance.

[1] Due to its unique coat colour, long mane and exceptionally noble pace, the Freesian has been a horse exclusively belonging to Lords for a long time.
[2-3] At the beginning of this breed there was a horse called Justin Morgan. It is a highly universal horse, used for saddling, hard agricultural work and teaming.

[4-5] The Haflings are vigorous and strong horses with a beautiful appearance, especially because of their light mane, which contrasts with their coat color.

The dressage of teamed
horses requires a lot
of rigidness and patience.

The mechanization followed by the motorization of agriculture early in the 20th century was almost responsible for the disappearance of the draught horses. Thanks to a few passionate team lovers, the tradition has remained up to today. The constantly growing competitions are attracting more and more participants.

The competitions are divided by the number of the horses in a team and include three disciplines: dressage, marathon and cones. The dressage begins with an introduction where the body posture and the beauty of the horse are classified including the cleanliness, of the harness and the elegance of the carriage. The dressage test follows with the required exercises – trot, pace, rounding and the rein back. The marathon occurs within a limited time on a 20 – 30 km (12–20 miles) long track divided into five sections, where three of these must be trotted at different speeds and two walked. The trotting sections contain natural barriers. The rider must demonstrate their mastery while bypassing the barriers and trees, crossing the water streams or passing through narrow gates. If they leg-touch the ground, unhitch or turn over the carriage, they receive penalty points. The timed hurdle race takes place in a large outdoor arena with a narrow and meandering track aligned with wooden bridges, walls and fords. Some horse breeds are better for teaming than others, such as the Dutch Friesian, British Hackney, Lipizzan and the American

Tradition and rules
of carriage driving

Morgan; from among the ponies, the best are the Welsh Mountain, Shetland, Hahlinger and the French Landais. The rules allow the use of different horse breeds for teaming; however the horses must have matching coat colors.

[1-2] Horse harnesses are usually made from well treated leather.
[3] The Dutch Warmblood is a good teaming horse. It has very springy or even extravagant pace which is well suitable for competition teaming.

[4-5] The Holstein is a jumper but it can be perfectly trained for teaming as well.

[1] The teams with ponies.
[2] For Britons, a pair usually rides the team.
[3] The Canadian Trottingbred breed is often used for teams.

[4] Two Friesians warm up before the combined dressage test and the team riding.
[5] The Welsh Pony breed is also used for teaming.
[6] The Norwegian Fjord is a very obedient and easily controlled horse.

[1-2] No dress is specified for partaking in the riding and dressage of the teams.

[3] The Welsh Cob is a pony originating from the cross-breeding of Celtic ponies with Arabian thoroughbreds.

[4] The skittish Welsh Pony often wears blinkers.
[5] The Morgan is a North American horse, most often with a black coat color.

151

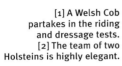

[1] A Welsh Cob partakes in the riding and dressage tests.
[2] The team of two Holsteins is highly elegant.

[3] As the name suggests, the Connemara pony comes from the Connemara lake and peat bog region in Ireland close to Galway.

Dressage horses

[4-5-6] The teamed carriages differ from each other – they can hold two, four or six passengers.

153

[1 and 6] The marathon is a timed competition which is highly attractive for spectators as the horses and teams must pass through fords. Very rigid carriages are adapted for this race and equipped with disk brakes. The riders wear helmets because the carriages often turn over or falls occur.

Dressage horses

155

Jumping horses

A key discipline of the riding sports is the fence jumping, which is very popular, undoubtedly because of their attractiveness and the diversity of the competitions and hence, they are not monotonous neither for the spectators nor riders. They are highly demanding for the horses, which need to demonstrate their bravery when standing face to face with the fence, their power, tractability, balance and speed.

The training requires perfect harmony between the rider and the horse based on quality dressage and real cooperation. The first riding competitions took place in the late 1860s in Ireland and France. Their success was huge and it was decided to list show jumping on the agenda for the Olympic Games in Paris in 1900. The technique of the riders, however, limited the fence height: they sat at the back, weighed down the horses and made them lose their balance. Around 1930, the French colonel Danloux, while teaching at a riding school in Saumur, came up with the idea of forward seating with a free pelvis as the American and Italian riders did. The principle of

Show jumping

forward seating has changed only slightly up to today. Presently, depending on the competition type, an official track holds six to fifteen mobile fences, either vertical or wide. The vertical elements are fences, walls, planks, hurdles and rails. The wide elements are brooks, oxer jumps and spa rails (from the lowest to the highest cross-bar height) where the latter mentioned require both high and long jumps. In fact, the difficulty is not the size of the fences but their deployment. Getting over the fences on a zigzag track is not comfortable but a chain of further fences allowing just one or two steps in between requires proficiency as well as good balance and flexibility.

[1] The riders accompany their horses with their effort.
[2] The horse's legs are protected downwards so as not to be injured when making contact with the crossbar.

[3] In the jump, the horse stretches, flies across the fence with its legs bent to the maximum.
[4] The riders are about to mount.

[1] Landing behind the fence is very sensitive. [2-3] The success of the jump depends on the approach to the fence.

[4] A perfect horse jump;
the horse looks like it's flying.
[5] The cooperation between
the rider and the horse is most
important when jumping.

[1] Jumping over a wall is very
difficult because this often
frightens the other horses
en masse.

[2 and 5] During the first modern Olympic Games held in Paris in 1900, the show jumping competitions included long distance jumping and high jumping. In 1912 in Stockholm, a complete competition that was split over three days took place. Each day was assigned to a single competition: the dressage, the endurance test and the show jumping where the rider had to demonstrate the required mastery with the horse. Since that time, these three disciplines have been listed in the agenda of Olympic Summer Games.

[1-6] At "Horse of the Year" which attracts many people in England, the horses with awards from previous events are presented.

[1-2] The best riders compete at the show jumping in Hickstead, England.

[3-4] After jumping over the fence, the rider raises their hand to prepare for the next one.

Together with the dressage and the versatility competition, show jumping is one of three riding disciplines listed in the official agenda of the Olympic Games. Alternately with the Olympic Games, the World Show Jumping Championship take place.

In between these two prestigious competitions, horse riders may regularly compete at the World Cup competition (held every year in winter) and at the Cup of Nations (also held every year). At national level, the official show jumping competitions are divided into classes A, B, C, and D depending on the quality of the rider. There are many show jumping competitions. For those marked with A, the jump execution is decisive. Every mistake "costs" a penalty point. A dropped fence or a hoof in the water when jumping over a brook means four points down, the first refusal three points down, the second six points down and the third is the eliminatory one.

The puissance competition takes place under this denomination. The track must contain four to six easy fences, at least one wall or a vertical element of a height of about 180 cm between them. In the case of equal results for the first place, a new shorter timed race is rode called the "jump off."

The "C" competitions should demonstrate the horse's speed. The official rules say that "the track must be meandering and comprised of various fences." This category includes the hunting competition where errors are converted into extra seconds and the speed and mastery competitions. Special competitions include the "American competition" which ends after the first error, the relay, the competition against the clock and

The full program

"choose the points" where the rider must choose point earning fences, of which the number depends on the fence's difficulty, within one minute.

3 [1-2-3 and right page]
Great achievements are
possible after years of
training and cooperation
between the horse and rider.

1 [1-2] Alexandra Ledermann from France at the Olympic Summer Games in Atlanta 1996.

174

[3] Show jumping has been an Olympic discipline since 1912.
[4] From left: At the Olympic Summer Games in Atlanta, Willi Melker (SUI) won silver, Ulrich Kirchoff (GER) won gold and Alexandra Lederman (FRA) won bronze medals.
[5] The joy of Ulrich Kirchoff (GER).

[1-2-3] A horse is disturbed by crowd noise and movement of things and the people around must not feel the rider's anxiety.

[4-5] Millions of spectators watch the riding competitions at the Olympic Games. The most popular is the show jumping.

177

[1 and 5] The rider on Airbone, which was born in Florida at the Montecillo breeding station, whooshes down the hill at Silk Cut in England.

178

[6 and 10] So as not to fall and pull the horse with them, the rider must retain a vertical position on the steep hill at the Silk Cut Derby.

179

[1-2] The Show Jumping World Cup takes place annually; here you can see the jump over two crossbeams.
[3] In 1996, Might Blue was chosen as Horse of the Year; here pictured with Robert Smith, the rider.

[4-5-6] The riders are afraid
of jumping over the wall.
Each brick down means
a penalty point.

181

To be good at jumping over fences, the horse needs to have a suitable body constitution, short, flat and muscular chine, firm hocks, back and deep hearth girth. The horse must be of a calm nature. Therefore, the Selle Français or the French Trotter, the German Trakehner and German Holstein are preferred instead of the somewhat restless English or England-Arabian thoroughbreds.

However, the supreme horse of this discipline is the Irish Hunter. It is bred mainly in Ireland and England and was originally used for hunting. It shows superlative powers and bravery.

In show jumping, ponies are considered as excellent due to their distinctive hindquarters which allow them to suppress the crossbar without a run up. They are competitions especially reserved for them and divided into four categories: "A" category – the smallest ponies, the Shetlands; those competing in the "D" category can have a height of up to 147 cm (58 inches). The best jumpers are the Welsh, Haflinger, New Forest and Connemara ponies.

The secrets of excellence

Of course, the natural qualities are not the only ones: hard training is required to develop balance, power and speed. The fence free training is aimed at teaching the horse to walk straight on a flat track and a track with curves and to immediately respond to the rider's command. Long riding at a canter helps the horse to strengthen its muscles and improve breathing, whereas the fence training teaches the horse to correctly spread its movement and to manage walks for rebounds and landing. The horses participating in the Olympic Games and the World Championships should be at least nine years old. The other official international show jumping competitions accept horses with a minimum six years of age.

[1-2-3] The Holsteins run freely on meadows before perhaps starring at a famous competition.

185

[1-2] The Tyrol (Austria) is the region where Haflingers are bred.

[3-4-5] The Haflingers have a small noble head and dark eyes proving their Arabian origin. The characteristics for this breed is their wide and light pace, kindness and resilience.

2 [1-2 and right page]
The New Forest ponies love
the moorland with its frequent
strong wind without having
to bother about flies and
other insects.

[1] An England-Arabian mare with a foal on a meadow.
[2] Two one-year old England-Arabian stallions.

[3] The Akhal-Teke stallion of a buckskin color.
[4] This Welsh mare has lighter coat colour than her mother.

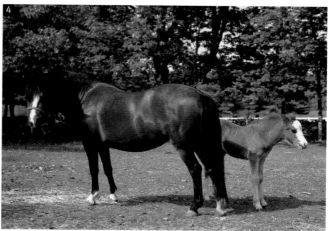

2 [1-2] Black riding cap, dark jacket and white trousers – the required dress for show jumping riders.

[3-4-5] The most interesting moment is conquering a brook (Badminton competition).

193

This race originates from former military competitions used for testing the horse's endurance in order to be included in cavalries. Until 1902, the races were 30 – 700 km long. Then, the French army decided to organize a more complex competition including dressage, a course over roads and pathways at a 48 km distance, a steeplechase and a jumping competition.

The competition was open to civilians and World War II did not change its form at that time. Depending on the horse and rider category, it can take one, two or three days. At the international level, it begins with the dressage, a series of requi- red figures during which the rider and horse pair must demonstrate their flexibility and elegance. The cross chase, undoubtedly the most interesting and difficult event follows.

A track between 4 and 7 km long covers fords, small hills, thic- kets, stretches, and contains

Eventing

approximately thirty dreaded fixed natural or artifi- cial hurdles: slopes with or without fences, ditches sometimes four metres wide, a "piano" consisting of a series of wide and variedly high stairs where several jumps have to be completed one after the other, troughs with shelters to be passed between, walls etc. Of course, falls and refusals receive penalty points as well as exceeding the specified time limit. The horse is eliminated after a third refusal of the same hurdle. In most cases, about one third of the riders are eliminated or drop out at this stage of the competition. The remaining horses must attend the final event – hurdle jumping – where the power and flexibility remai- ning in the horses can be demonstrated.

[1-2-3] At Badminton, the riders are particularly afraid of crossing the water right behind the hurdle.

[4 and 7] Crossing of the trunks dispersed on the slope requires a speedy run-up to cope with the hurdle.

[1-2-3] The riders rush the horses to the very spectacular jumps to get over all the hurdles.

[4] At Badminton, the spectators gather at the highest hurdles; they snap pictures of the horses looking as if they are flying out of there.

[1] This hurdle is very difficult for the horses as they have trouble estimating the clearance distance.
[2] The last stretch follows on from clearing all the hurdles.

[3-4] The Burghley competitions are very spectacular; they take place in a park of the chateau that was owned by Lord Burghley, the paymaster of Queen Elizabeth I.

202

Jumping horses

[1 and 6] The Burghley hurdles are very original; most are made from trimmed yew trees or straw. Their highly rustic appearance increases the difficulty of the track which contains 13 hurdles.

[1-2] The terrain in Burghley is rippled, which increases the difficulty of the race.

[3-4-5] The winners of the Burghley competition receive, in addition to a lot of money, a Land Rover from the company organizing this event.

Badminton, Burghley – one
of the prestigious locations
that makes England a country
of jumping.

A nglo-Saxons dominate in the versatility competitions both in teams and individuals. At the Olympic Games, the gold medals have been shared between the English and New Zealand riders for many decades followed by the Americans and Australians.

The famous Mark Todd from New Zealand won the gold medal twice (in 1984 and 1988) and won bronze in 2000. In 1996, the gold medal went to his compatriot, Blyth Tait with Ready Teddy after winning bronze in 1992. Two Britons – Leslie Law and Philippa Funnel – stood on the winner's podium next to the American, Kimberley Severson in Athens in 2004. In the team CCE (concours complet d'équitation = versatility riding competitions), Germany and France surprised everyone several times when the latter won at the Athens Games. However, these are always exceptions to the rule… The horses of great Anglo-Saxon champions undoubtedly differ. They are fast, persistent and brave and have all the qualities needed to cope with a demanding endurance competition. In addition to the Olympic Games, the best riders meet at CCI**** (the four-star competitions at premium level). There are four competitions in the world: in the USA – Lexington (The Rolex Kentucky Competition), in Adelaide (Australia) and two in Great Britain with the most difficult and most extraordinary competitions in Badminton and Burghley. The Anglo-Saxons demonstrated their excellent quality there as well. Surprisingly, the winners were – if we put the Americans aside for the jumps – the Germans, the Dutch and the French to a lesser extent.

On the winners' podium

[1-2-3] In the top level competitions in England, such as in Badminton and Burghley, only a few riders other than Britons break through. The Germans have surprised everyone several times but this was with riding English horses.

3 [1-2-3] This high hurdle still covered with leaves is very difficult for horses that are new to jumping over it.

210

[4-5] The riders use scarce stretches to improve their times.

[1-2] Non-Britons come to attempt to break through in the Badminton competitions but they are usually all Anglo-Saxons such as New Zealanders or Australians.

[3-4-5] The jumping horses must be fast, persistent and particularly fearless. They must have absolute trust in their master and vice versa.

[1 and 5] The winning riders of the famous Badminton races become celebrities quickly. The Queen, a passionate horse lover, acknowledges them in most cases.

2 [1-2] All horses have their legs protected by foam pads.

[3-4] After a jump, the horse needs a lot of power when often having to gallop in muddy water.

2 [1 to 4] The Anglo-Saxon hegemony rules over women as well. Many female riders join the dressage.

218

3

4

[1-2] The elegant dressing of the female riders match the horses.

Jumping horses

[3 and 6] Both the appearance of the horse as well as the technical movements are equally important during the dressage.

Recreational
horses

The horse trips resemble
cowboy adventures to
the trippers.

Horse riding trips are an integral part of "green tourism" and as such, they have been attracting a constantly growing number of people since the 1960s. You don't need to be an experienced rider to enjoy a short mountain, countryside or a seaside horse ride. Just a few hours is enough – this is one of the reasons why so many people take up this activity.

Only a little experience is needed to participate in rides for several days or several weeks under the guidance of a skilled professional who can handle the route selection as well as all material problems. These long term tours require the good physical condition of both the rider and the horse as the daily distance travelled can be up to 30 kilometers (20 miles). The tours are usually divided into groups according to experience levels. The beginners walk on sturdy and calm semi-ponies and the others trot or canter on the thoroughbreds. In France, most centers providing these tourist trips are concentrated in the southwest mountain areas. In Great Britain, the promised land of riding tourism, there are many camps on large areas in Ireland, Wales and Scotland. Of course, nobody can stop you from leaving Europe and daringly going to Mongolia, to the Canadian Rocky Mountains, to the Moroccan Atlas or in the manner of those famous travellers who undertook such great journeys as the Coquet

Horse trips

sisters (from Paris to Jerusalem in the 1970s) or Stéphane Bigo who travelled from Turkey to Afghanistan during the same time period.

[Left page and photo down] The hard and exhausting work of the cowboys is far away from the myths from the Hollywood movies with John Wayne. Today, the West plains are crossed by Mexican immigrants as herd guardians.

[1-2] The large grazing lands of the US West can be crossed only by horses.

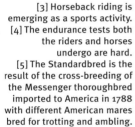

[3] Horseback riding is emerging as a sports activity.
[4] The endurance tests both the riders and horses undergo are hard.
[5] The Standardbred is the result of the cross-breeding of the Messenger thoroughbred imported to America in 1788 with different American mares bred for trotting and ambling.

[1-2] Horses love water, they like trotting and galloping on beaches. In Deauville, many horse rides are organized.

Recreational horses

[3 and 6] The routes of the endurance competitions lead are along forest pathways and brooks.

231

[1-2-3] The horse ride allows the experienced riders to enjoy the riding as well.

[4-5-6] A whole family can take a horse ride with calm and well trained horses to places not accessible by car or on foot.

233

[1-2] During the times between competitions, St. Moritz (Switzerland) offers family horse rides in the snow covered countryside.

234

[3] Despite its predecessors, this Arabian thoroughbred loves snow trotting. In addition to the pleasure derived from the activity, the leg muscles strengthen because of the power the horse has to produce when running in the powder snow.

Germany, Belgium and Scotland have banned fox hunts and this ban is to go into effect in Ireland and England despite the protests.

The real riding sport is the hunts that have a long tradition in Anglo-Saxon countries; riders follow a dog pack and can gallop at high speed and around many often difficult natural obstacles, barriers or ditches. Unlike in France, the objective of the hunts is to catch the cornered animal. The hunter's day begins very early in the morning when the dog handlers walk around the forest to find out what animals are there. The leader and the crew members are informed of this in the morning. Depending on the animal to be hunted, a specialized pack is compiled to pursue the animal until it gets tired and is captured. An animal equipped with strong protective features has a chance to win four times from five attempts. This mainly applies to roebucks of a subtle constitution and it is the best at disorienting and shaking off the dogs like no other animal.

A hunting horse has to have many qualities, of which the most important is balance: it is expected to pull through often dug up forest paths, ruts left by vehicles usually covering traps. The horse needs to be persistent, untiring and very calm so as not to be scared by dogs and hunting horns. For the hunts, the most often used horse is the Selle Français. The Anglo-Arabian is suitable as well, but the ampleness is somewhat missing.

Hunts

[1-2-3] Undoubtedly, England is home to the hunts. Recent banning of hunts aroused many debates between animal protectors and supporters of tradition.

[Right page] Cooperation between the dog pack and horses is required for hunting.

[1-2-3] Fox hunting is most popular in England. At the hunt's end, the landlord gives a cup to the participants.

[4] For Britons, the hunt is
a means of a gathering for the
common passion that is a horse.

4

[Left page a 1 - 4]
The dogs hunt down the animal. The pack structured around its leader detects the location of the fox or deer. The rider and his horse chase the pack consisting of about twenty dogs.

243

Game horses

The sport known as "the sport of Kings and the King of sports" is one of the oldest games ever; it was played over two thousand years ago in Persia. In China and Japan it was considered effective training for war combat; the sport then "conquered" India and right there, in a small north east Manipur province, the British colonists discovered it.

The English colonials established the first European polo club in 1859 with rules that are still applicable today. Since that time, polo has come to England and in the 1870s, polo conquered the USA and Argentina, which – due to their top class riders and famous Criollo horses – have been dominating this sport for decades.

Two teams of four stand against each other on a field approximately 250 meters long and 140 meters wide. The aim of the game is to score maximum points by hitting a willow ball into the goal of the opponents using bamboo mallets. The polo rules attempt to maximally protect the riders and horses: to avoid collision, it is prohibited to cross the path of a player, to hustle an opponent, to sandwich him or shoot the ball in front of the front legs of the opponent's horse. The game is divided into eight, six or five parts (chukkas), lasting seven and a half minutes each. This fast and colorful sport, rode at a canter, is very tiring for the horses – therefore at international events, the riders change horses after each part. In addition to

"The sport of kings"

having great resilience, a polo horse must have strong hocks and good stability; it must be able to change rhythm and direction quickly. All these properties are met by the sprightly and self-confident Argentine Criollo breed which resulted from cross-breeding with English thoroughbreds.

[1-2] A polo horse must be able to stop from full speed, if the rider so wishes.

Game horses

[3-4-5] Polo is a sport with two teams of four. The game has five, six or eight parts, each lasting 7.5 minutes.

3 [1-2-3] The Argentine polo horses are the best.

[4] The game of polo requires the ability of excellent horse control as well as accuracy for hitting the ball.
[5] The polo helmet has a special shape based on old colonial headgear.
[6] To avoid accidents, the legs of the horse are protected by protective pads. The tail is also protected and tied.

251

[1-2-3] Polo is the oldest team sport in the world. The very first reference to this impressive riding sport is 2,500 years old and comes from Persia. Later, it expanded into India where it was discovered by the English.

[4-5-6] In polo, each player has a position and a function. Number 1 is a forward. They must score the maximum. Number 2 helps Number 1 but is a defender as well. The most important player is Number 3 – they take the best shot, return the ball back to the game from the rear line and take the penalties. Number 4 is the defender. Their goal blocks the opposing team's players and plays the long balls.

253

1

2

3

[1-3] Tough horse lunges have a strong grip; the rider can stand on the horse as well. [2] Each rider has their own mallet set.

Game horses

[4-5-6] Polo has penalties like in football. There are four penalty types. The worst faults are punished by penalties taken at an empty goal – the opponents must gather behind the goal. Less serious faults are punished by penalties against a guarded goal – in this case, the opponents may stand between the ball and the goal.

2 [1-2-4] Polo requires horses which do physical exercises daily or at least four times a week.

Game horses

[3] After the game, the riders and the horses take a shower. [5] Horseshoe maintenance is necessary for fast and sharp polo movements.

257

[1-2-3] The big polo teams relocate with large semi-trailers transporting both horses and food. The horses, riders and the horse tenders make up a large team.

[1-2] The polo ponies
in the Argentine pampas.

[3] Resting polo horses
in a meadow.

Game horses

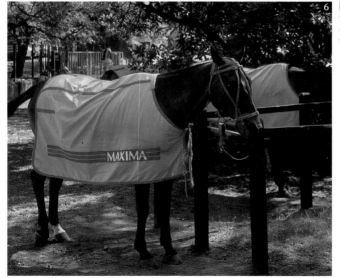

[4-5-6] Before the game, the Argentine horses are covered with covers bearing the owner's name.

To ensure the equality of the polo teams as far as their chances are concerned, the players have handicaps ranging from −2 to +10. The team handicap is achieved by the total of all the individual handicaps. In the game, the weaker team is awarded a number of points in advance equal to the difference of the handicaps. The best polo players may win two international prizes.

The prizes are the Coronation Cup and the World Cup, which has attracted thousands of spectators since its establishment in 1987. The best teams are Argentina and Brazil; both have won the title three times.

As the classic polo game requires large areas and a lot of money, derivative games to make polo more accessible were developed. In principle, the rules are the same but the distances and the number of players is less. Paddock polo is played on a field 100 x 50 metres in teams of three. The mallets are still made from bamboo but the ball is leather or rubber. Indoor polo has the same rules but is played in a hall. Australia gave birth to polo-cross which does not use mallets but long-handle racquets similar to those used in squash. Children can join the junior polo tournaments on smaller fields of which the dimensions differ according to

Polo games

the ponies used: these are 40 x 20 metres for category A players saddling Shetlands ponies, 30 x 20 metres for category B players and the category C players play in the paddock polo fields. In 1995, the first snow polo games took place in Megève.

[1-2] Each year, a big polo tournament takes place in Windsor Park in England where the Queen's Cup is awarded.

[3-4] It also happens in England that the national teams are beaten by the South American teams.

[1-2-3] In Argentina, the polo games attract thousands of spectators. The popularity of polo is only second to football in Argentina.

[4-5] Undoubtedly the Argentineans are the best polo players. Since winning the 1936 Olympic Games, Argentina has been building the world's best teams.

LA NACION

[1-2-5] Polo is played internationally; this is a game in St. Moritz in Switzerland where the Cartier World Cup is awarded. [3-4] South Africa has become an important nation from the polo point of view.

[6-7-8] In Sussex, England, there is a big golf course in Cowdray Park as well as the polo field that is famous for its games.

[1] Polo has its Nations Cup where England and the Netherlands dominate.
[2] Prince Charles is passionate about polo. One competition bears his name.
[3] One trophy was named after Prince Philip.

[4-5-6] The polo riders use very special equipment. The helmet is equipped with a protective grid and they have reinforced knee pads, gloves and zipped leather boots. They use mallets with bamboo handles. The ball is made from plastic.

From a bouquet game to Argentine pato, many riding competitions provide the opportunity for gauging horse balance, skills and speed. Horse-ball, which is very popular today, has two teams of four players who must pick a medicine ball up from the ground using six handles and pass the ball to the opponent's basket, fixed three meters above the ground.

Due to the girth under the horse's abdomen and to which both the stirrups are attached, the riders can bend down to the ground. This intensive and very sporty game (two half-times, 10 minutes each) was invented in France around 1970. The game was probably inspired by Argentine pato where two riders attempt to pull out a leather bag with a duck (pato in Spanish) until one gives up. The winning team then gallops away pursued by their opponents who try to steal the prey. For safety concerns, the game was banned in 1882 and re-appeared again in the 1930s in a form very similar to horse-ball.

For generations, the Camargue guardians were devoted to various local games: we can mention the bouquet game originating from a court tradition when the riders fought for a bouquet to be offered to their lady; the orange game where the rider on a galloping horse had to catch an orange held by a female citizen of Arles or the ribbon game where the keeper attempted to pull out the ribbons of his opponents while protecting his own single ribbon.

The Aiguillettes game, stemming from the Middle-Age tournaments, is widespread in France (the aim

Other games

is to catch the rings hanging on the bracket using a lance), whereas push-ball is more widespread in Anglo-Saxon countries (the ponies have to push a giant ball into the opponent's goal). We can also mention Gymkhanas, which can also have a relay form, where it is necessary to zigzag between the posts or barrels located close to each other as quickly as possible.

272

[1-2-3] A show called "team penning" stems from the traditional activity of cowboys when they used to brand the livestock with a red-hot iron.

[4-5-6] "Team penning" takes place in a corral full of small calves which need to be lassoed within a specified time.

275

[1-2] The "team-penning" competitions take place across the USA and also in Europe, particularly in the Camargue area.

3

[3-4] "Cattle Penning" is similar to "Team Penning"; the only difference is the performance of a single rider going only for one animal. The rider must sort out the herd and enclose the one and only animal that is numbered or marked with a colored collar into the corral.

4

3 [1-2-3] "Barrel Racing" is a speed riding event around metal barrels. A pair consisting of the rider and horse must zigzag as quickly as possible around three barrels making a triangle together.

[4-5-6] The rider may choose whether to start their ride with the barrel on left or the right hand side. They can touch the barrels but must not fall. The horses passing sharp bends at high speed must demonstrate great agility and the ability of impressive acceleration.

279

3 [1-2-3] Here in St. Moritz, the skijoring was presented at the 1928 Olympic Games and it almost became an Olympic discipline.

[4-5-6] When the skier and their horse dart at full speed onto the snowy planes, they can exceed 60 km/h.

3 [1-2-3] "Horse-ball" is new among riding sports; it uses a leather packed ball with handles that the players use to catch it. The game is for two teams of six riders and everybody attempts to score a basket as in basket-ball.

[4-5] This discipline uses the horse's weight, especially when it is necessary to catch the ball at full speed or when the ball should be pulled up and scored with.

283

The Shetland ponies are
the best for children's
riding sports.

P ony games, joining fun with useful-ness, are a perfect opportunity for children to relax and acquire the riding basics. Similar to exercising in an arena, they can learn to control the speed, find the right seating in the saddle and gain more agility and ease. However in the games, the technique is not the goal, just a means to achieve better results.

The joy and desire to win, which makes children go in search of the technical issues they have to cope with, is the most important here. The pony games emerged in the fifties in England and in France, they appeared forty years later. In French riding centers there are about thirty pony games played today. These are team games organized in relays – the slalom, the game of two cups (where it is necessary to pick up the first cup on a pole and put it on another one and then do the same with the second cup), and the game of five flags, the bottles game and the box game. In the rope game, the first rider must zigzag on the start line with a rope in their hand to the back line where the second rider is awaiting them. The latter must catch one end of the rope and both the child-ren must return slaloming back to the start line. The slalom tracks are very frequent in the games in order to help the children to learn to switch the direction. In the tournament game, the first rider must hit a target with a lance, give the lance to the next rider to hit the target as well and then give the lance to another rider and so on. The other games

Pony Games

use horses only partially. An example is the bag running race or "a foot, a horse" where one half of the track is covered on horseback and the second on foot.

The participants in the pony games are divided into the age categories of mites (for the youngest), juniors and cadets (adolescents). The senior cate-gory is for adults.

284

[1-2-3] In England, at the Olympia Shetland Grand National, young riders between 9 – 12 years old compete in an extraordinarily difficult hurdle race.

[4-5] Even though this race is a children's race, bookmakers accept high bets. Nevertheless, many of these competitions are for charity.

3 [1-3] The "Mounted Games" usually take place outdoors.
[2] In the cup game, a child must grasp a cup on a pole and put it on another one without breaking it within a specified time limit.

[4 and 7] The program for
Windsor Park in England
lists many skill exercises.

289

[1-2] For increased difficulty, the cups are sometimes put on very thin poles.
[3] One of the difficult skill games is the one of placing the balls into the baskets.

[4-5] Although the hurdles are very low in the Shetland Grand National, getting over requires a great riding skilfulness from the young riders.
[6] The Mounted Games organized in Windsor Park include the slalom, the ball, the cone, the five flags, the box, the rope, the two flags, the cups and the postman competitions.

Exhibition
horses

In a circus, the horse dressage
acts are considered the most
prestigious.

I t is surely not an exaggeration to say that a circus would not exist without a horse. The great story of the originally called "riding theatre" began on the impetus of Philip Ashley, a colonel in the British army and an excellent groom who put together a riding performance in 1768.

The performance, initially consisting of vaulting, high school and horse pantomime (hipo-dramas) acts, was completed by clowns, tightrope walkers and jugglers because of Ashley's fear of boring the audience. However, the soul of the performance was a horse and the horse remained the soul of all circuses until the end of the 19th century when wild animals took their place. The horse was overshadowed but not removed from the arenas as was demonstrated by five generations of the riding vaulters, acrobats and jugglers of the Gruss family. The horse acts presented by the family brings an uncommon emotional experience: the horses react freely without any pushing, just only to music, voice and the trainer's gestures and do sophisticated choreographies, walk backwards, on their back legs, or move in excellent harmony to the rhythms of the waltz.

The vaulting is a sui juris discipline today and official competitions are held regularly. The animals have a vaulting surcingle with a cloth on with which the acrobat performs an excellent routine requiring both balance and gymnastic abilities. In the competitions, there are six required figures: the position "sitting on the horse with hands crossed," the standard (the kneeling rider has an outstretched leg and the opposite arm for four walks), the mill (the rider is riding side-saddle, on the left and then on the right, with legs stretched

A riding theatre

out and lifted to his/her face), the side-saddle, standing and scissors. Following the required program there is the free riding which usually contains poises and breathtaking somersaults.

[1-2] In a circus, the horse dressage acts are the privileges of large families such as the Gruss family in France.

[3-4] In a circus, commanding the horses in German is a custom. The big quirt is used only for suggesting a movement, never for hitting the horses.

[1-2] In the arena center, the trainer makes the horses to turn around in the arena, very close to the audience.

298

[3] Women are also great horse trainers.
[4] A rider standing on several horses jumps above the galloping horses.

299

[1] An excellently trained horse can perform astonishing movements such as kneeling-down.
[2] Three horses dancing to music.

[3-4] On the command of a circling quirt, the horses rear and remain rearing until the trainer gives another command.

The Bozkashi, the Tauromachy, Hungarian Post, Fantasy, Rodeo, and more – across the world, experienced riders often pursue dangerous but always spectacular riding demonstrations that are in most cases derived from old agricultural or war practices.

For thousands of years, the Central-Asian riders have been fighting in many merciless battles, the Afghani bozkashi requiring both riding talent and bravery. After the start, fifty horses congregate around the goat leather on the ground, prancing against one another until a rider succeeds in picking it up. Insane and unbridled hunting then follows as the opponents attempt to grab the prey. The winner is the rider who can outrun the excited herd and succeed in throwing the goat leather into a circle drawn in an area reserved for the game.

In Hungary, Post or Puszta-five is very popular. One rider stands on one horse while riding five or ten cantering horses. Considering the abilities required it is no surprise the same riders are listed in the records of the winners of the international teaming competitions.

The Tauromachy, which became famous on the Iberian Peninsula, has different rules in Spain and Portugal. In the Spanish corridas, the horses with picadors act in the first part only. In Portugal, they are present through the whole event and the task of the rejoneadores is to demonstrate a real riding show including high school elements, the piaffé, the levade etc. before they lock horns with the bull. The horse suppresses its natural fear due to an absolute devotion to the rider that is achieved during a long and strict dressage. The Andalusians

Horse performances

and the Portuguese Lusitanos, resulting from the cross-breeding of the Andalusians and Arabian horses, achieve great results in these arenas.

[1-2-3] The riders in a standard dress show the dressage of the Andalusian horses.
[Right page] A horse performing Andalusian bowing.

[1-2-3] Hungary offers many riding shows; the standing rider controls five horses at once.

[3] The Hungarian riders in their traditional dress.

4

5

[4-5-6] This rider wearing traditional Hungarian dress, shows his ability to let the horse sit, get down and kneel.

6

3 [1-2-3 a Right page]
In rodeos, the driver must avoid sitting for as long as possible in the saddle of a wild horse while holding on with one hand.

[1-2-3] These female acrobats demonstrate vaulting on a galloping horse.

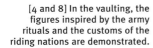

[4 and 8] In the vaulting, the figures inspired by the army rituals and the customs of the riding nations are demonstrated.

[1] Horses sleep while standing. If injured or incapable of standing on their own legs, they have to be held by a harness.
[2] A trained horse plays football with its trainer.

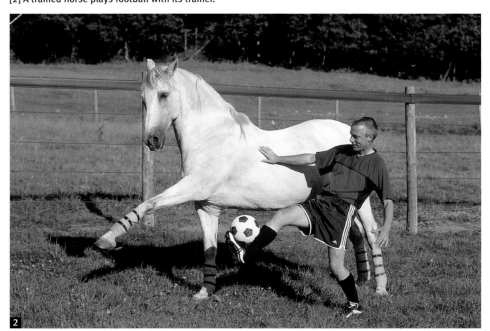

Work horses

Today, the former breeds
of the work horses attend
tourist or sporting events.

I n the West, the horses were imperative for work until 1900 – 1950. In towns and countryside they transported both people and cargo. They hauled all possible machine types: ploughs, gates, mowers, harvesters, tilting carriages with manure and more.

They experienced a cruel life in mines where they hauled carriages with coal in underground corridors. The happier ones left the corridors in the evening and returned back to their stable but the others did not and consequently went blind. Railway, the invention of the combustion engine and tractors released then from their heavy duty, however this also posed a risk for their breeding. Fortunately, several passionate breeders founded associations to prevent their extinction. Today, there are nine breeds of work horses in France: the Ardennes, the Auxois, the Boullonais, the Breton, the Normandy Cob, the Comtois, the Percheron, the Trait du Nord and the Mulassier du Poitou. The Percheron with its light grey coat which is highly valued abroad for its elegance is the result of a complicated improvement in the heavy breeds. The Black Percheron was cultivated as well, and is sought after in Japan. On the other side of the English Channel, the Shire is very popular. You can recognize it due to the long hairs on its legs and its extraordinary height (up to 190 cm!). The horse can haul a five ton cargo. Together with the Percheron, the horse is a phenomenal success at fairs and exhibitions. From among the heavy breeds, let us not forget the Freiberger from Switzerland, the Clydesdale from England and the Friesian from the Netherlands, which was the most common work horse for centuries throughout Northern Europe.

Cart-horses

The work horses are used for carting wood only marginally; they are mainly used for recreational riding, team competitions and hauling competitions where they are yoked to sledges bearing a cargo of several hundred kilograms of cast iron.

[1-2] Ploughing with beautiful work horses which appears during the festivities as something quite beautiful when recalling the traditional methods used in agriculture.

[3-4] The Freiberger is a new breed of riding horse from the Avenches (Switzerland) the former Freiberger work horse is also known as the Franches-Montagnes and was widely used across Switzerland for the agricultural work prior to mechanization.

319

3 [1-2-3] Plough the most regular furrow in the shortest time – this is the task of the competitors using the old ploughs. The jury also assesses the horse harness.

[4-5-6] These work horses wearing beautiful harnesses demonstrate the work their predecessors did before the arrival of tractors.

[1-2-3] In Belgium, the work horses used to haul heavy logs. Today, they compete in competitions where the winner is the horse able to haul the heaviest cargo.

322

[4-5] Horses are still used for wood carting in many countries of eastern Europe, particularly in Romania.

1 **2**

3 [1] The Belgian work horse can haul sleds holding up to twenty passengers.
[2] The Percheron hauls the sleds in snow without problem.
[3] The Haflingers are small but robust horses.

[4-5-6] There are several breeds of Belgian work horses for sled hauling, e.g. small, medium and big Belgians.

The American West, from the Mexican to the Canadian border, is the place where a great legend was born: the cowboys. These wild defenders of ancient tradition, aloof to the hard competition of intensive breeding, today mostly live in Utah, Montana and New Mexico.

The cowboys of today have their horses available from ranch owners. The life of the cowboy is closely associated with the changing of the seasons. In spring, thousands of cattle are gathered and taken to the summer grazing lands. In autumn, the animals are taken to the winter pastures. During the "dead season," the cowboys return to the ranch to repair houses, take care of the animals, brand the calves and train for the next rodeo western competitions. An ideal horse for a cowboy is the Quarter Horse which has no competitor in terms of training and as far as in rushing the animals, finding a lost calf or preventing the herd from disintegrating. The breed originates from the horses brought to the New World by the Spanish conquistadors in the 16th century and later cross-bred with English thoroughbreds. The horse is stubborn with an extraordinary temperament. It has a compact muscular body with a strong back which makes it fast at a canter for short distances; this gave it the "Quarter" name according to a quarter mile, i.e. 400 meters. The guarding of herds is not a privilege only for the American cowboys; the Camargue guardians, South American guachos and Hungarian stockmen live almost the same lives.

Cowboys

326

[1] Herd guardians standing watch.

[2-3] Many horses used by the cowboys came from bicolour or dun breeds that the American Indians used for hunting buffalo.

[1-2-3] Although Jeeps or helicopters are used by large farms to guard their animals, the owners still like horse riding on their estates.

[4] In the West, the Palomino horses are a full breed. In Europe, this name stands only for a coat colour.
[5] Cowboys riding Paint Horses and American Buckskin.
[6] The Paint Horse breed is very popular with cowboys.
[7] The cowboys on the horses are always accompanied by dogs.

[1] The lasso is an indispensable work tool for the cowboys.

[2] The calves held in the corral are separated and captured by lasso in order to mark them.
[3] The "team penning" competition.

[4 - 7] To recall the golden age of the Wild West where the horse ruled, all small towns of the American West organize rodeo competitions, the barrel races etc.

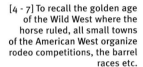

[1-2] For the barrel racing, great skill and accuracy is required from the riders.

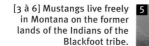

[3 à 6] Mustangs live freely in Montana on the former lands of the Indians of the Blackfoot tribe.

[1-2] The horses are marked so as to identify their owner. [3-4] The traditional outfit of the cowboys includes leggings, spurs and lasso.

[5] The lasso is used for catching stray animals or animals distanced from the herd.

337

Although there have not been any wars fought on horses in the West since 1918, horses are still members of various armed forces, for example the famous English Horse Guards or the horses of the Canadian and New York police. In France, there are the Republican Guards shows during the celebrations of 8 May, 11 November and the national holiday on 14 July.

The Republican Guards organize great parades on horses and on foot on the avenues of the capital city. The cavalry regiment has about 500 horses, mainly the tall Selles Français (170 cm in average), divided into three squadrons by the coat color: the first includes the chestnut horses, the second the light bay horses and the third one, the dark bay horses. The brass band uses chestnut horses except for the kettle-drum players who ride grey horses. The riders attend riding exercise shows such as "La Reprise des Tandems" (Eight riders with sixteen horses) or "Le Carrousel des Lances" (33 horse riders with spears) and the best ones attend the international dressage competitions, the versatility and jumping competitions. Throughout the year and in addition to their military and official activities, the cavalry guard the forest lands in the Paris area and the coast line, especially in summer. Several years ago, army horses became very popular in France again in the rural police where they occupy an elite position. Formerly, the horses were appreciated for their speed and resilience but today for their convi-

Army horses

viality and their friendliness to the environment. As the rural police are, among other things, charged to guard natural areas and forests, it was absolutely natural to (partially) abandon their cars and motorbikes and set an example for the public... In eastern France, people have rediscovered horses when recruiting the junior brigades within the local police patrols.

[1] The Queen of England inspects the saluting squadron from the horse's saddle.
[2] Prince Charles and Prince Philip receive the salute from the army at a ceremonial show.

[3] The Royal Guard passes the Queen to salute.

[4-5-6] The show of the Royal Guard in front of the Royal Palace in London is a show zestfully watched by tourists as well as citizens of London.

341

[1] Buckingham Palace is guarded by policemen on horses.
[2] The cavalry of the Royal Guard parades with swords drawn.

[3] The English cavalry has its own trumpets. Formerly, these riders signalled the attack.

[4] The Horse Guards provide protection to the Queen and the royal buildings. In the building of the Horse Guards in Whitehall, close to the residence of the Prime Minister are the headquarters of the Royal Guard and this building plays the role of an official entrance to Buckingham Royal Palace.

[1] The Horse Guards belong to two of the oldest regiments of the British army, the Blues and Royals and the Life Guards.

[2-3] The arrival of the Queen followed by Prince Charles and Prince Phillip for the inspection of her troops.

[4] Dignified guards with their characteristic helmet.
[5] The Queen on her horse inspects her troops.
[6] The Horse Guards consist of 350 men. Men selected for the Horse Guards service must attend riding training for four months before they go to the parades.

[1-2] Each troop of the Blues and Royals has its own "*drum horse*," a rider with two kettledrums on both sides of the saddle.

346

[3-4] The royal escort of the English royal court has been accompanying the kings since 1660. Today, it is escorting the Queen.

[1] The Royal Guard.
[2] The Blues and Royals.

[3] The Horse Guards escort the Queen, the Princes Charles and Philip and the Duke of Kent.

[4] The Life Guards in Whitehall.
[5] The arrival of the Queen is announced by the trumpet of the Blues and Royals.
[6] The parade of the Blues and Royals opens the procession.

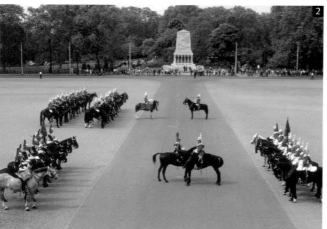

[1] The brass band of the Royal Guard.
[2] The ceremonial changing of the guard in Whitehall is a great tourist attraction.

[3] In the royal stables is the Royal Carriage,
here towed by 12 horses in ceremonial harness.

3 [1-2-3] The Canadian police on horse parade at an official ceremony.

[4-5-6] Today, the Royal Canadian Mounted Police is the equivalent of the French national gendarmerie.

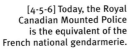

Horse careers

An extraordinary foal may appear in the breed despite its parents being common horses.

Breeders, Riders – two professions, both done with love and which are both rewarding and demanding. The breeder, either the director of a private stud farm or a farm manager, usually focuses on a single breed and offers its animals for sale.

There is a long way to go before the horse gets to the market – in most cases, the mares do not leave the stud farms before their fourth or fifth birthday with the exception of thoroughbreds commended to a trainer at their age of around two. The breeding of the thoroughbreds is too expensive and remains reserved for a privileged few. Patience is thereby needed for the others... As for the tasks of the breeders, they can look quite frightening: mares in heat they must present for the coupling or insemination, to help the mares in foaling, to choose a stallion, to wean the foals or train them for riding, as well as to keep the stud farm in order, to feed, groom and even train the horses. Even with the help of a stable boy or a groom, most breeders do not know what a Sunday or a holiday is... What's more, to compensate for all the costs of the above activities, they must (at least during the first periods) complement the horse breeding with cattle bree-

ding because of the advantageous and immediate profit. Formerly, there were the autodidacts on the breeding market but the breeding and insemination techniques have improved to a level that now requires attendance at a special school.

And – should the breeder's life look like a soldier's life, what can be said about the life of a professional rider? Their presence at renowned competitions requires an adequate horse. How do

Breeders, Riders

you get this when all the great horses are commended to only the great and talented riders? Only a privileged few succeed in escaping this vicious circle and the others must focus on horse sales or teaching.

3

[1] In the stud farms, many women work as grooms.
[2] The boxes usually have a low door to allow the horses to poke their heads out.
[3] During competitions, many breeders transport the food for their horses in the semi-trailers attached to an off-road vehicle.

[4] A chewing horse.
[5] For many breeders, each horse has the right for a blooming flower in front of the box.
[6] The rider is the last link in the chain of people taking care of the horses.

[1] A rider on a hurdle race in Badminton.
[2] Covered horses returning back to the stable.
[3] A rider galloping on his Arabian thoroughbred.

[4] Polo players in action.
[5] Michael Stoute, the famous stable owner.
[6-7] Riders at the dressage competition in Badminton.

[1] A newborn foal leaning on its mother.
[2] A dressage competition with a Friesian.

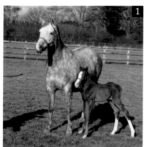

[3] Horses in a meadow.

[4] A Pinto horse rearing during dressage.
[5] A Friesian running freely across the meadow.
[6] The mares of wild ponies give birth in the wild.

363

The work of horseshoer has changed over time. In the past, the horseshoer was an indispensable inhabitant of a village, who changed the horse shoes for the towing animals that were worn and torn because of the work. The horseshoer also helped the blacksmiths to produce the harness because nobody else had better skills when working with metal.

The horseshoer also worked as a blacksmith and a locksmith. When the towing horses disappeared from the paths and fields, the horseshoers had to retrain. Many of them became devoted to bodywork and some found their places in riding clubs. The contemporary horseshoer has to know how to work with various materials such as alloys, aluminium, plastic and polyurethane that has tended to replace iron and the glue that is slowly replacing the nails. The comfort of the horses has improved as well. As the riding sports have recently considerably diversified, new horseshoeing was necessary: new horseshoes for skijoring and snow polo were developed onto which special snow claws or plates could be hammered. The horseshoer must be able to produce horseshoes for all hoof types and must often make adjustments for balance, limping and to facilitate walking. In case of locomotive problems the horseshoer will call a vet to adjust the horseshoe together such as the patient's condition requires.

Only one vet in a hundred specialises in horses. These vets must know both traditional and sports medicines. They are an important element of the "racing chain," they look after the horse's health before the race and recondition them again after

Blacksmiths and veterinarians

the race. They give advice to the breeders about the food, vaccinate and regularly vermifuge to avoid the most serious diseases. In the case of a problem, the vets are called out to help a mare with foaling.

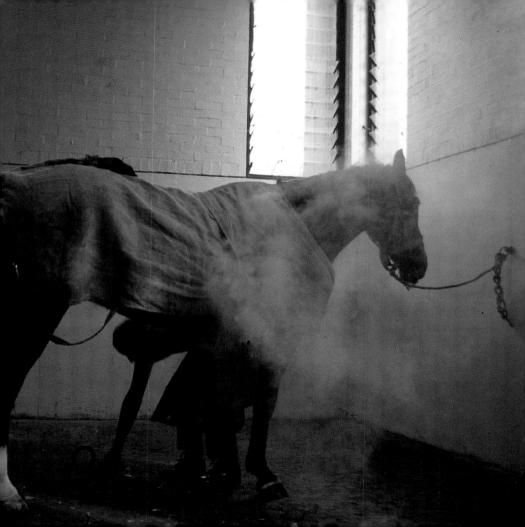

[1-2-3] Prior to the horse shoeing, the hooves need to be well cleaned and rasped in order to hammer a hot horseshoe.

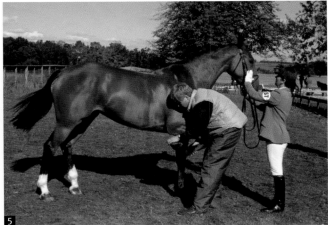

[4] The horseshoer removes the old horseshoes using tongs.
[5-6] The vets often inspect the horse's limbs which are their most fragile and important part.

367

[1-2-3] Formerly, each village had its own horseshoer. Today, the profession is back again due to the development of riding tourism.

[4 and 7] The vets use ultra-sophisticated medicine, particularly in the case of racing horses.

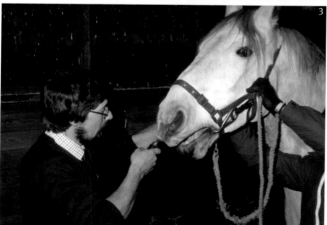

[1-2-3] The vets also work as dentists because the horses suffer from teeth pain just like humans. This vet is scraping the teeth of a horse.

[4] The vet checks the condition of the horse's legs before leaving for a race.
[5] The vet examines the horse after a demanding race.
[6] The vet listens to the horse's heartbeat after an intensive performance.
[7] The vets also check the lather of the horses.

371

The stable boy is certainly not an insignificant person in the stables. He takes care of cleaning the boxes, cleaning the horse's hooves, brushing of the coat and mane and also feeding. He observes both the mental and the physical condition of the animals and can spot the first signs of a problem much better than others.

In the event of illness or injury, he administers the medicine prescribed by the vet, changes the bandages or guides the horse on the long walks as part of the rehabilitation program. The main workplace of this dedicated man is the stable so that the horses can establish a close relationship with the boy and some horses can even waste away when the stable boy has to leave. The boy usually takes care of ten animals. The day starts at 6 a.m. with the distributing of food, cleaning and greasing the saddles and harnesses and cleaning the boxes. His work is interrupted by giving three or four feeds and it ends late in the evening with the last check of the horses. If everything is okay, he will have some time to ride his favourite horse for one or two hours, however in small farms where there is the maintenance of the riding house, paddocks and meadows is required, there is no time for any riding.

The grooms at the racing stables may be, in addition to the traditional work of the stable boy, charged with transporting the animals and warming them up on the racecourse before the races. At the end of the day, after the race, they

Stable boys and grooms

take the horses back into the stables. If talented, they often become close helpers to the trainers or go on to become trainers or stable managers themselves.

This profession is usually performed by young stablemen with a CAPA (certificat d'aptitude professionnelle agricole) certificate received from a specialised school or training institution.

[1] The breed owner spends a lot of time with his horses.
[2] A Quarter Horse walks with its groom.

[3] A horse carriage decorated with the prizes awarded.

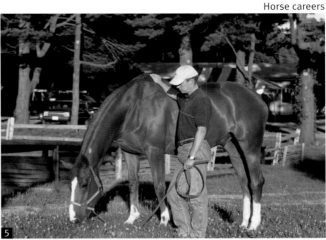

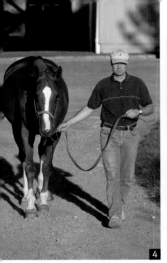

[4 and 7] The groom takes out a horse from the stable, lets it feed and grooms it. The groom usually performs this work twice a day.

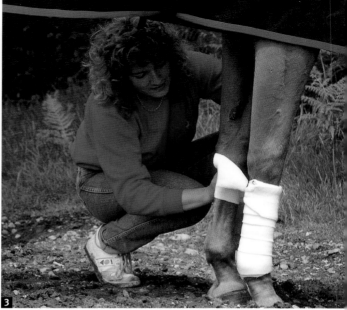

[1 and 4] The task of the stable boy/girl is to take care of the horses, groom them, clean the hooves and bandage the legs.

[5] A female groom leads the horse trotting.
[6] The ponies walk away guided by a groom in the polo game.
[7] A groom takes a horse to a meadow.

[1-2] After training, the stable boy washes the horse.
[3-4] The stable girl rewards the horse with a snack.

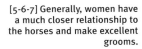

[5-6-7] Generally, women have a much closer relationship to the horses and make excellent grooms.

[2] The stable girl takes care of threading the horse's tail.

[1-3] The horse cleaning equipment: brushes and currycombs.

[4] Before the polo game, the ponies are allowed to gallop in the wild.
[5] A horse likes flowers as a reward that it – of course – eats.
[6] The horse ride starts very early in the morning.

[1-2-3] The horse feeds mainly on grass when it grazes in a meadow but the champion horses have a diet consisting of corn, oats and granules full of vitamins.

[4] Oats additives are usually supplied to the foal-caring mares.
[5] In the stables, the horses are mainly hay-fed in wintertime

The development of sport and tourist riding brought with it a boom in the riding centers as well as a large growth in the numbers of teachers and guides. A guarantee for success in this area is a sense of pedagogy and long riding experience, but that's not all.

Indeed, the role of "teacher" includes three categories of trainers in the sport disciplines: instructors (first level certificate), senior instructors (second level certificate) and chief riding instructors (third level certificate). Difficult tasks are often assigned to them where teaching has only marginal importance. The latter are the managers who must adopt the services offered to the requirements of the public, check the club cleanliness as well as the acceptance quality, to determine the pedagogic content, to plan all activities, to manage a team of instructors, to ensure and check the renewal of horses and to pay attention to the safety of children as well as adults.

Two major institutions provide supervision over the riding tourism providers - Fédération des randonneurs équestres français (French Federation of Riding Tourism Providers) and Délégation nationale au tourisme équestre (National Delegation of Riding Tourism). The responsibility of the riding guides is huge as they look after the complete course of the tour. It includes planning the tour in advance, managing the accommodation and boarding for the riders and for the horses. During the tour, it can happen that the treatment of a horse will be required; they must know how to treat limping, respiratory problems and other symptoms of the horses. The basics of horse medicine are necessary.

Teachers and guides

The guide is expected to demonstrate leadership abilities: the guide must provide evening entertainment and develop the tourist aspects of the trips; hence the guide must know all about offering the customers a visit to tourist attractions or various cultural events.

[1-2-3] During the riding lessons, children learn riding and to respect the horse.

[4-5] From the very first lessons, the riders learn how to control their horse to jump over the barriers; here there are simple wooden bars on the ground.

[1 and 5] Children learn many activities in the riding centers; not just horse riding but they must also learn to take the horse out of the box and bring it to the river.

[6 and 9] The riding lessons for children are usually provided by very competent instructors requiring strict discipline from the students.
[10] In the riding schools, the riders learn how to feed the horses.

Horses
in the wild

This foal of only a few days
of the old breed of English
ponies lives partly in the wild.

The foals pullulate in spring after about eleven months of gravidity. Birthing of the foals is always a moving spectacle, however it is one not often seen as mares usually give birth to foals in the night, in a quiet and well covered place. Foals (the term for horses up to six months) come into this world with their front legs first.

The head and the back then follow. After the foal is out, the mother licks the foal to clean it, warm it up and discover the foal's smell. After several inevitable awkward and unsuccessful attempts, the newborn finally stands up. It starts looking for a papilla to drink the treasured colostrum, the first milk which is rich in antidotes and proteins. During the first week, it suckles every fifteen minutes and starts to taste the grass from the meadow. At about four months of age, the foal is able to graze properly but still needs the milk for development. In the wild, the foal may suckle until eighteen months or two years but the breeders usually wean them in their six months. More or less, the foal is brutally weaned from the mare. So as not to traumatize the foal by this expe-

Foals

rience, the foal does not remain isolated from the other horses and learns to live in a society. After some adaptation time, it plays with other foals of the same age, kicks up its heels, prances, chases after the other foals and friendly bites the others. Also, this life in the group has its own rules.

Towards its elders, the foal behaves submissively; this behavior is called *snapping*: if an adult horse (or a man) is approached, it opens and closes its mouth with its neck stretched forward and moves its ears. This ritual usually ends at three years of age; for male horses with a more developed domination instinct, the ritual often ends earlier than for the female horses.

[1-2] The Dartmoor ponies have their body constitution adapted for children's riding – due to their moderate character they are used as initiation ponies and used in all disciplines.

[3-4] The Dartmoor mares are fertile; they have excellent milk-yielding and in 99.9% of cases they feed their foals themselves. These ponies usually live for a long time. In most cases, they are indispensable throughout their 30 years.

3 [1-2-3] The Gelderlands, also known as the horses of Gueldre, are bred in the central Netherlands and in 1875 originated from Oldenburgh, England-Normandy horses and local horses. Today, the breed is endangered.

[4-5] Rare Dulmen horses today live in the Merfelder Bruch reservation in Germany. They emerged from the cross-breeding of the wild horses of that region with domesticated horses, which likely re-adopted the life in the wild. Texts from the Middles already mention these horses. The breed is endangered.

397

3 [1-2-3] The foal of the Hanoverian spends its life in the wild with its mother until a strong and very enduring jumping horse originates from the foal; they are excellent at hurdling and in dressage.

[4-5] The Freiberger or Franches-Montagnes is the only Swiss breed. The foals move well on the mountain paths; for that matter, "Freiberger" means "they who easily pass the mountains." After training, it will be a good-hearted and obedient outside horse.

[1] This Exmoor foal belongs to the oldest British breed.
[2] This mare and foal is the Groningen breed. They come from the Netherlands and are now becoming endangered.

[3] The Andalusian has the nickname of "a noble horse."

[4] This Dartmoor pony has the same discolorations as its mother.
[5] The suction, which means contact with mother, gives the foal a deep feeling of safety.
[6] The Hungarian thoroughbred is mainly bred in Montana.
[7] The coat color of this mare and her foal is the same.

[1-2-3] The Dartmoor pony
has its childhood in the wild
on the Devon moorlands.

4 **5**

[4-5] The Welsh Cob is a small, sturdy and stocky horse with a fine head. It has retained the hardiness, the resistance and the strength of the pony and the conformation, the speed and the very brilliant action of the horse.
[6] The first walk of a foal with its mother.

6

[1-2] The dark coat of the Falabella foal contrasts with the coat of its mother.
[3] Foals of the same age like to play together.

[4] Foals always stay close to their mothers.
[5-6] The grace of the Andalusian is already obvious with the foals.

3 [1-2-3] The coat color of a foal and its mother is not always identical. With many breeds, the foals have a dark coat that turns lighter with age.

[4] The mare licks the foal after the birth.
[5] This Shetland pony instinctively knows how to suckle its mother.
[6] The coat of the Paint Horse camouflages the foal in the moorlands well.
[7] The Morgan is a highly elegant American horse.

[1] A foal needs only a few minutes to stand up.
[2] Foals like to lie down; when adult they will spend most of their time standing, even while sleeping.

[3] The Arabian foal has the body constitution of its breed: it is a fine, elegant thoroughbred; it has a short chine and flat back (it has less vertebras than the others), a more or less dish shaped face, big eyes, small ears, fine and thin legs and a high tail often worn up with panache.

[1-2-3] Depending on the stallion used for coupling with the Arabian mares, the foals that are born can be divided into three morphological types according to experts: kehailan, muniqi and siglary.

[4-5] Newborn foals stretch their front legs as they are not very stable at this time.

The coat colors are closely related to the age, size and breed and represent something that could be called "an ID card" of a horse. The coats are simple or composite and exist in an infinite diversity of colours, ranging from jet black to the lightest grey through bay, chestnut, and piebald, roan. A code system was used for classification of the types.

The simple colors have the BANC code (white, chestnut, black, white coffee) whereas the composite colors are divided into two sub-categories: BIS (bay, dun, mouse grey) which indicates a monochrome coat ending with black horsehair; the GAL coat (grey, strawberry roan, buckskin) forms the mixture of two horsehair colors. The piebald and roan colors defy this classification; they are the mixture of black, white and red hair.

Similarly to the Australian Brumby, the Selle Français or Icelandic as well as some breeds of ponies and horses may have all the coat types with one colour – most of the Selles Français are chestnut. Many breeds can have any one color – such as the thoroughbred, the Quarter Horse, Italian Salerno, Holstein or Trakehner. The Appaloosa, bred in the USA, can be distinguished by its solely spotted coat. For the horses of a primitive breed, the dun coat is most frequent with tints of yellow. The horses can also be identified by the uniqueness of their faces and legs: the stripes, the

Coat colors

white marks on bridge of the nose are large, unconnected or short. The spots covering the face are known as "bald face" and "star" is the white mark in the form of a diamond between the eyes. The socks that are widespread with thoroughbreds are the white marks over the hoofs. When the marks reach the knees, they are known as the stocking over the knee.

[1] The coat of the New Forest Pony is always monochrome, usually bay.
[2] This young Trakehner has a white stripe on the lower leg part. It is called the sock.
[3] For Halflingers, the coat color contrasts with the mane color.

414

[4] The horses coat color is abbreviated as: AP for appaloosa,
BA for bay, BL for black, CH for chestnut, DB for dark bay,
DC for dark chestnut, DU for dun, GR for grey, LB for light bay,
PA for palomino, PB for piebald, RO for roan.

4

[1-2] The Holsteins have a white spot on their heads called stripe marking.
[3] The acceptable coat colors for the Lusitano are grey, bay and black. The most beautiful horses have a highly shiny coat.

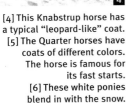

[4] This Knabstrup horse has a typical "leopard-like" coat.
[5] The Quarter horses have coats of different colors. The horse is famous for its fast starts.
[6] These white ponies blend in with the snow.

417

[1] A newborn Icelandic foal.
[2] Exmoor ponies have a bay, dark bay or mouse color.
[3] Dartmoor foals in the wild.

418

[4] The Holsteins have stripes on their legs.
[5] The coat of the Groningen foal goes very dark later as for all types of this breed.
[6-7] This mare, foal and ponies have a piebald color.

[1] This Gelderland mare has the features of the body colour on the muzzle; these are the bare patches.
[2] The American Pinto often has a piebald coat color.
[3] This Andalusian has a very light coat.

[4] This stallion has a piebald coat color; the Anglo-Saxons call it paint.
[5] This Exmoor pony has a bay coat color.
[6] This foal has an appaloosa coat color. It is white with black spots.
[7] The golden mane of the Haflingers is a characteristic feature of this breed.

[1-2-3] The piebald or paint coat colors are highly desirable for exhibition horses. The color is frequent for ponies and small ponies.

422

[4] The coat color of this stallion is "blue roan," i.e. it is black or brown-black and spotted with white hairs giving the horse a blue tint.
[5] This Belgian horse has a monochrome coat.
[6-7] It is normal for monochrome parents to have foals with a spotted coat color.

[1-2] The black coat, especially when shiny, is one of the most sough after colors.
[3] The grey coat of the Andalusians is usually spotted with white blemishes.

[4] This horse has white socks on all legs and a stripe on its muzzle.
[5] The highly rare and valuable black Andalusian stallion

425

The released Holsteins released run with complete freedom.

I n the wild, the herd instinct appears with a horse. As a nomad, horses can travel long distances to find their pastures. The horse herds consist of several "families" of which the undoubted leader is the breeding stallion.

His task is to keep the cohesion of the group and during their travels he prevents the disintegration of the herd and keeps his mares away from rivals. His leading position has several advantages: he is the first to drink fresh water when the herd finds water and he has the best resting place. Some foals sometimes dare to invade his territory but a single kick is usually sufficient to drive the off. The colts leave their families at about two or three years of age either alone or driven away by the adult stallion. They then join the other young stallions of the same status. They entertain each other with pretend fights and wait for the fillies to be the "head of the family." These games teach them to protect their position inside the group. In their adult age, they retain their playful temperament. Hustles, tags, pretend runs against false danger – it all comes in handy when they want to have a fun!

The horses are very expressive and can express their emotions and moods in 1001 different ways. Their small movable ears are particularly most telling – when aimed forward, it means the animal is confident and attentive; aimed backward means dissatisfaction or pain; when distanced from each other and relaxed, they demonstrate boredom. Their voice has many nuances as well: a horse neighs to locate distanced herd members, snorts in the event of danger, sighs when satisfied and exhales forcibly to frighten a rival etc. Its affection is demonstrated during the grooming: from top-to-tail like two partners scratch each other backs. To summarise, although the horse cannot speak, their body says everything.

Breeding in the wild

[1] The Camargue live in the wild in the Rhone delta river.
[2] The Sicilian is an especially sturdy horse and well resistant to fatigue.

[3-4] The Icelandic feels good in any terrain.

3 [1-2-3] Most horses are not afraid of winter and can be outdoors all year long. Running on snow improves their limb muscles.

[4-5-6] On a snow-covered meadow the horses dig into the snow with their hooves to reveal the grass they love because it is saturated with water.

1 **2**

3 [1-2-3] The ponies in Norway spend most of their time outdoors. Temperatures of up to -40°C do not prevent them from playing in the snow.

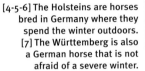

[4-5-6] The Holsteins are horses bred in Germany where they spend the winter outdoors. [7] The Württemberg is also a German horse that is not afraid of a severe winter.

[1] A mare licking
her newborn foal.
[2] Spring is here and first
Holstein foals are birthing.
[3] The salty areas are
home to the Camargue.

[4] A Freiberger mare and foal on a spring meadow.
[5] This Hanoverian foal rests on a meadow in Germany.
[6] The Hanoverian was originally bred for the cavalry and teaming.

[1] A small Shetland
suckles its mother.
[2] This Falabella foal
does not leave its mother.
[3] This herd of Haflingers
chews fresh grass.

[4-5] The Camargue are always grouped. They form a "manada."
[6] Young horses like grooming each other.
[7] All horses love water as it helps them to get rid of their parasites.

437

[1-2-3] The beauty and pace of the Andalusians is at its best when that are able to run freely.

[4] This Holstein neighs.
[5-6] Horses galloping in the wild. Trotting is not a natural pace for a horse.

[1] The Norwegian Fjords like life in a herd.
[2] This Haflinger stallion chews spring grass.
[3] This Arabian horse builds up its muscles in the snow.

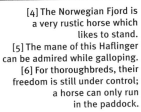

[4] The Norwegian Fjord is a very rustic horse which likes to stand.
[5] The mane of this Haflinger can be admired while galloping.
[6] For thoroughbreds, their freedom is still under control; a horse can only run in the paddock.

[1] A foal following its mother.
[2] Shetland ponies are often closed in pens on the moorlands.

[3] A Paint foal (which indicates its colour as well) with its mother on a meadow.
[4] A foal of wild pony looking for its mother.
[5] The Andalusians also behave haughtily in the wild.

[1-2] These foals have a piebald or paint color. Today, these horses with their spotted coat colour are a special breed. Formerly, they were Quarter Horses.

[3] This beautiful Haflinger stallion can be distinguished by his tail and his white, fine mane. It is common to see Haflingers with very long manes on both the sides of the neck. He has a white stripe from the forehead to the nostril.

[1-2-3] Wild horses live in herds and love the presence of other horses.

[4-5] In fact, wild horses are the offspring of local horses which returned to the wild.

447

This distinctly spotty coat
is one of the main features
of the Knabstrup.

C razy positions, curious mimicking – sometimes horses assume positions invoking our curiosity, arouse our tenderness or make us laugh: a mare stepping with her leg into a muddy puddle and then lying down around it, a young foal jumping around its impatient mother and those horses who charmingly greet each other with their nostrils.

A stallion suddenly stretches its nostrils and purses its lips, a pony squinting to show that everything is fine or dominant male horses defying each other at a parallel gallop. And, at the start of all this funny behavior there is the seduction ritual. A male horse capturing the smell of a mare in heat stretches his head upwards and turns his lip up which looks as if he is smiling. This position (the "flehem reaction") is assumed by all horses smelling a special or unusual smell. The male horse starts to swagger before the female horse and neighs loudly. The beautiful female horse is not interested and in this case, she loudly snorts to signal her unfriendly opinion.

Funny horses

And then there are the horses that provoke or entertain because of their unusual mark of nature or their special coat colour or because people dress them strangely for ceremonies or traditional festivities.

Then they march through the streets before the admiring eyes of their human friends, decked out with weird hairdos and accessories – woven tails and manes, spotty feathers on their heads, artificial fringes preventing them to see, opulent or strange harnesses.

[1] For foals, contact by mutual licking is very normal.
[2] To remove parasites, horses like roll on the grass.
[3] The rear legs allow the foal to scratch.

450

[4-5] These young Hungarian Horses are playing. These games are the origin of the real fights when the mares are in heat.
[6] This Freiberger foal tries to neigh.

3 [1-2-3] In Camargue, copulation occurs in the wild. The stallions often fight over a mare.
[Right page] This Haflinger stallion has a white blaze, mane and tail

[1] When a horse rears up it is to impress another male horse. [2] This beautiful American horse has a creamy coat.

[3] In the wild, the Friesian is a fast and elegant horse.
The black coat with much horsehair became a feature
of this breed (horses being the bearers of the chestnut genes
are identified and mercilessly rejected from reproduction).

[1-2-3] The Camargue live in herds called "manada" under remote human supervision.

[4-5] Two Camargue fighting together.

[3] [1-2-3] The stallions of the Norwegian Fjord are carefully selected, especially by their coat color.

458

[4-5] The Norwegian Fjord is very old breed; they w ere the Viking horses.
[6] A Paint Horse rears up.
[7] All horses love water; some much more than others and they will not hesitate to lie down in it with their rider.

Index

PHOTO CREDITS

All the photos in the book by **Only Horses Agency**

Except for these on pages: 14 [2] ; 15 [4] ; 45 [4] ; 48 [2] ; 118 [1 and 2] ;
136 [1] ; 140 [1] ; 141 [5] ; 160 [1 and 2] ; 161 [3 and 4] ; 166 [1, 2 and 3] ;
167 [4, 5 and 6] ; 175 [4 and 5] ; 176 [1 and 3] ; 177 [4] ; 336 [1, 2 and 3] ;
337 [4 and 5] ; 428 [1 and 2] ; 429 [3 and 4] ; 446 [1, 2 and 3] ; 447 [4 and 5] ;
456 [1 and 2] ; 457 [3, 4 and 5]: **Claude Poulet**.

Photo on the cover: **Horizon Features**.